CODE NAME
HABBAKUK

D1021290

CODE NAME HABBAKUK

A Secret Ship Made of Ice

L.D. CROSS

VICTORIA · VANCOUVER · CALGARY

Copyright © 2012 L.D. Cross

All rights reserved. No part of this publication may be reproduced, stored in a retrieval system or transmitted in any form or by any means—electronic, mechanical, audio recording or otherwise—without the written permission of the publisher or a photocopying licence from Access Copyright, Toronto, Canada.

Heritage House Publishing Company Ltd.
www.heritagehouse.ca

Library and Archives Canada Cataloguing in Publication
Cross, L. D. (L. Dyan), 1949–
    Code name Habbakuk: a secret ship made of ice / L.D. Cross.

Includes bibliographical references and index.
Issued also in electronic format.
ISBN 978-1-927051-47-4

    1. Habbakuk Project. 2. Aircraft carriers—Design and construction—History. 3. Ice strengthened vessels—Design and construction—History. 4. Military research—Alberta—Patricia Lake. 5. World War, 1939–1945—Naval operations. 6. Pyke, Geoffrey. I. Title.

V874.C76 2012   623.825'5   C2011-908611-5

Series editor: Lesley Reynolds
Proofreader: Liesbeth Leatherbarrow

Cover art: Dominic Harman, www.bleedingdreams.com

The interior of this book was produced on 100% post-consumer recycled paper, processed chlorine free and printed with vegetable-based inks.

Heritage House acknowledges the financial support for its publishing program from the Government of Canada through the Canada Book Fund (CBF), Canada Council for the Arts and the province of British Columbia through the British Columbia Arts Council and the Book Publishing Tax Credit.

 Canadian Patrimoine Heritage canadien   Canada Council Conseil des Arts for the Arts du Canada   BRITISH COLUMBIA ARTS COUNCIL

16 15 14 13 12   1 2 3 4 5
Printed in Canada

This book is dedicated to all those original thinkers who will not let their imagination be inhibited by present-day conventions and who have the determination to persevere in the face of ridicule, anger, bankruptcy and perceived failure.

"I have not failed. I've just found 10,000 ways that won't work."
—THOMAS EDISON

Contents

Prologue

IMAGINE A SEA BATTLE. *They had prepared for it in endless exercises, but this was no dress rehearsal. The attack had been going on for hours with bombs exploding all around. The sound reverberated and amplified inside the belly of the ship, deafening many of the men. Two torpedo strikes had already damaged the hull, with one hit opening up an exterior compartment.*

This was not supposed to be happening. They were the ones to launch surprise attacks against enemy submarines and land bases. They were to escort naval convoys of merchant ships carrying essential supplies for the Allied war effort. If the shipping lanes were not defended, the war would be over, and the Allies would be on the losing side. Now it seemed that their ship—

the protector—needed protection. The crew worked frantically putting into play all the techniques they had practised so often under much calmer circumstances.

Sea water was pouring in through a hole just under the waterline. The compartment was filling up fast. If this new technology did not work as expected, they would all drown or be blown to bits when the refrigeration units with their miles of ducts became blocked and on-board fuel exploded. But something strange was happening. The hole seemed to be getting smaller. Water was freezing around the jagged edges of the opening and moving in to repair the skin of the hull. This stuff really did work. But could it keep ahead of the battering the warship was taking from both airborne and undersea projectiles?

While it looked like a flat-topped iceberg from the outside, it was an aircraft carrier inside, with all the planes, crew, fuel and munitions of the much smaller steel versions. And, it was said, because of its ice advantage, even with an exterior casing 36 feet (11 metres) thick, it would not sink. Super-cooled water could ice up any break in the vessel caused by attack or melting. But ice is brittle. What if it cracked and shattered in the middle of the ocean? Nobody wanted to bob around in the cold North Atlantic on a tippy ice floe hoping for rescue before they died from hypothermia. This probably was a crazy idea after all. Who dreamed up this stuff? But as planes took off from the carrier deck, the crew members down below noticed a strange phenomenon: when struck by shells or explosives, the outside ice skin held and started to repair itself. Craters caused by direct hits started refilling and self-sealing almost immediately. The crew remained safe inside their ice fortress. Obviously there was more to this ice ship than they had been told.

As the frustrated enemy withdrew to fight another day, the immense vessel set out for the nearest suitable harbour. Not just any harbour would do; the ship's colossal size meant only the widest, deepest ports could accommodate its draft. Even then, it would have to anchor offshore as smaller boats brought out cargo in semi-trailer containers and ferried soldiers and motorized equipment back to the coast. Accessing the ferry boats was no problem—the crew simply cut a huge hole in the side of their bergship and transferred supplies directly on board. If necessary, a short two-lane ice highway could be poured; the water would instantly freeze, allowing trucks and armoured personnel carriers to be driven off and transported to land by barge.

When work was complete, the ice highway was cut free, the cavity re-iced to its original thickness, and the intact ship set out for its next encounter on the high seas. It floated away like an immense ice island, appearing to be a detached chunk of Arctic glacier to even the most prying eyes. But this frozen white battleship was better than ice—or it could have been. Had it existed outside the imagination of an eccentric inventor, a determined prime minister and an aristocratic naval officer with royal connections, Project Habbakuk could have changed the course of the Second World War.

1

Desperate Times

IT CAME TO BE KNOWN as the Battle of the Atlantic, and it was the longest continuous military campaign of the Second World War. Starting in 1940, German U-boats (meaning *Unterseeboot*, literally underwater boat or submarine) attacked convoys of ships ferrying supplies across the North Atlantic Ocean. When a U-boat sighted a convoy—and who could miss a fleet of slow-moving, weakly defended boats bobbing in the cold waves?—they would radio their position to other U-boats that would then close in and wait until dark before picking off their targets. It was like spearing fish in a barrel.

The attacks of these "wolf packs" were lethal. On October 18, 1940, six U-boats attacked a convoy designated

SC-7 (departing from Sydney, Cape Breton Island) and sank 15 ships in six hours. The next day, three more U-boats joined the feeding frenzy, and that night 12 vessels of another convoy of 49 ships were sunk. The British Royal Navy did not have enough ships to protect the convoys, and those they did have were outgunned. In November 1940, the 37 ships of convoy HX-84 (departing from Halifax, Nova Scotia) were escorted by only one armed cruiser with guns that could not even fire shells far enough to reach the German attackers. The puny escort vessel and five merchant ships went down. The August 1941 Atlantic Charter, an agreement between British prime minister Winston Churchill and US president Franklin Roosevelt, meant convoys would also be protected by the US Navy. But losses continued. Between January 1942 and March 1943, seven million tons of cargo went to the bottom of the Atlantic. In July 1942 alone, 142 ships were sunk, and in November 1942 a total of 117 were lost to U-boat attacks.

By the winter of 1942, German U-boats had sunk more than 600 Allied ships in what was called U-boat Alley. Prime Minister Churchill needed to find a solution to the carnage or the Nazis would be victorious. It was decided to group even more ships together and hope for safety in numbers. Massed convoys of merchant ships left North America and started across the Atlantic with tons of much-needed food and war supplies for the citizens and armed forces in Britain. The drawbacks to these large convoys were the delays involved in waiting to assemble, the longer route often required, the necessity of matching the speed of the slowest ship and further delays caused by port congestion during unloading.

As an island nation, Britain depended on imported goods for survival. More than one million tons a week were needed to continue the war effort, and they could not come from German-controlled Europe. Steel and aluminum for munitions and equipment were desperately needed. Many of the supply ships were still being attacked and sunk, with devastating loss of life, by the U-boat wolf packs, which picked off slower ships and stragglers with their most effective weapon, the torpedo. The explosion of a torpedo as it slid underneath the keel of a merchant ship created a giant gas bubble that caused the ship to break in two. Therefore it was possible for a U-boat to sink even large or heavily armoured ships. Ships were being sunk faster than shipyards could build them.

During the Second World War, over 30,000 British merchant seamen were killed and more than 2,400 ships sunk, but the years up to 1944 were the worst in terms of casualties and cargo lost. Some 70 Canadian merchant ships were lost along with 1,600 sailors, including 8 women. It was small wonder that during the Battle of the Atlantic, the prime U-boat hunting area gained the nicknames "Atlantic Gap" and "The Black Pit."

The Allies needed a way to protect their shipping, and

they needed it fast. Conventional aircraft carriers were used to transport, refuel and provide takeoff and landing strips for older aircraft, but there were few of them, and they were also needed in the Mediterranean. Their outmoded flight decks were too short for the newer planes, and the below-deck hangars were too small for bombers. In addition, they were equally vulnerable to underwater attack by torpedoes and had great difficulty remaining stable in the heavy Atlantic waves. No plane could land or take off from a pitching and rolling flight deck, and many were forced to ditch in the ocean, further reducing Allied air power. Britain had nine aircraft carriers available early in the war, but by September 1939, two of the largest were no longer fighting in the Atlantic theatre. HMS *Courageous* had been torpedoed with the loss of 518 crew members, and HMS *Ark Royal* was recalled to port, as the risk to carriers from U-boats was deemed too high.

Nor could land-based air cover come to the rescue. There was a scarcity of aircraft for defensive support, and the limited range of patrol planes meant they could not get to where they were needed to protect shipping lanes. Or, if they got there, they would not be able to return to home base. The pilot had to ditch at sea, which was usually a death sentence. The mid-Atlantic air gap resulted in a desperate situation. The convoys remained easy targets, and the loss of supplies reduced any possibility of winning the war.

To compound the problem, the Allies were also drawing

up plans to invade Europe, and Churchill wanted large floating platforms to support amphibious landings on the continent. This meant that all ideas to avoid military catastrophe were considered—the more innovative the better. Far-fetched proposals that would otherwise have been rejected as science fiction, unorthodox, unreasonable or exorbitantly expensive were now carefully considered and analyzed. Some even made it to the design phase. Word went out from the British War Ministry that no recommendation was too outrageous to merit review. Nothing was off the table.

Canada was an integral part of the Allied war effort, and many Canadians experienced the deadly threats faced by convoys in the Atlantic. Among them was Clarence Decatur (C.D.) Howe, known as "Minister of Everything" in the government of Prime Minister Mackenzie King. When Canada entered the Second World War in September 1939, the War Supply Board, headed by Howe, was given extensive powers to direct arms production. Howe began a rearmament program to manufacture ships, planes, small and large arms, clothing, vehicles and other supplies for Allied forces. Canada's economy was transformed from an agricultural to an industrial one.

Howe, who became minister of munitions and supply, was personally introduced to the perils of the Atlantic Gap on his way to Britain with a group of officials, including Canadian businessman E.P. Taylor, to discuss supplying the

British war effort and coordinating the Joint Air Training Program to build 120 airports and instruct 131,000 air crew in Canada. While travelling in a convoy, his ship *Western Prince* was torpedoed in the early morning of December 14, 1940, by German submarine U-96. The order was given to launch lifeboats and abandon the disabled vessel. As the survivors bobbed in the icy water, there were flashes of light from the U-boat as its crew photographed the scene for proof of their kill. Then the U-boat captain took aim and fatally torpedoed *Western Prince* amidships, causing her to explode. Captain Reid had time for two farewell blasts on the ship's whistle before the waters closed over them. Sixteen lives were lost, including Reid's. The remaining 55 passengers and 99 crew members were abandoned at sea in flimsy boats with no motors. The U-boat skimmed within 50 feet (15 metres) of Howe's lifeboat, then submerged and disappeared.

The dynamic Howe took charge of his lifeboat with its 34 passengers and crew. Although seasick and freezing in the sub-Arctic waves, everyone was assigned a task as they rowed and bailed in hopes of making it to Iceland, some 200 miles (320 kilometres) away. They had meagre rations, thin clothing and a few distress flares that they sent up in faint hope of rescue. Death by exposure or drowning was their likely fate. The British Admiralty had issued a standing order that no merchant vessel was to stop and pick up survivors in an area where U-boats were known to operate.

The convoys were the thin lifeline that kept Britain alive and fighting, so were not to be risked on humanitarian missions, no matter how desperate the situation.

After eight bone-numbing hours, someone in a lifeboat spotted a ship. They could not believe their luck. Accompanied by an old First World War American destroyer for protection, the ship came near. After consulting with his officers, and with his crew at battle stations in case another U-boat appeared, Captain Dewar of the *Baron Kinnaird* placed his hull between the lifeboats and the prevailing wind. He knew about the Admiralty order, he knew there were U-boats in the area, and he knew there were survivors who would die if he did nothing. For him, it was a straightforward decision. Rope ladders were thrown down for the able-bodied, then baskets lowered to lift the injured on board. Within half an hour, everyone was rescued, and the ships set out for England by a longer, more northerly route, arriving four days later. Not only did he survive the long hours in a lifeboat, but after his interrupted trans-Atlantic trip, Howe proceeded as planned to negotiate the training program for pilots and an aircraft production program that would build over 12,000 aircraft by the end of the war. In an interview with the *Manchester Guardian*, he said he considered every hour that he lived from that disastrous day onward to be borrowed time.

For his heroic efforts, Captain Dewar of the *Baron Kinnaird* was relieved of his command by the Admiralty.

Howe and the other passengers of *Western Prince* collected money for the crew, but there was no way to properly thank Dewar for his bravery and sacrifice. They gave him a marine radio receiver as a very small token of their appreciation.

Canada's contribution to the Second World War would have been much less had C.D. Howe perished in the cold Atlantic on that gray December day. Howe would work with Dr. C.J. Mackenzie, acting head of the National Research Council, on many wartime projects, as well as post-war on the establishment of Canada's nuclear industry. For Howe's return trip to Canada, Prime Minister Winston Churchill ordered a Royal Navy battleship to take him safely home.

Howe's terrifying ordeal vividly illustrates why, in recalling his own wartime leadership, Churchill said, "The only thing that really frightened me during the war was the U-boat peril." In October 1941, he took action to address that and other threats when he appointed Lord Louis Mountbatten to be chief of Combined Operations (shortened to Combined Ops), an organization responsible to the Chiefs of Staff for the development of tactical offensive equipment and expertise that would win the war. Mountbatten's appointment changed the character of the department. He introduced unusual people with offbeat talents and ideas because he believed they prompted regular staff to think less bureaucratically. Militarily, he favoured deploying small specialist units that could innovate to develop new tactics, operate behind enemy lines and sabotage key installations in quick raids.

Mountbatten took personal charge of the raid on the German-occupied port of Dieppe on the northern coast of France in August 1942. It was a deadly fiasco that resulted in the loss of 4,000 lives. Some observers viewed the raid as an instructive rehearsal for a future invasion of Europe (the D-Day landing of June 6, 1944, called Operation Overlord), while others said the failure was a result of Mountbatten's youth and incompetence. The situation might have ended the military career of a less fortunate and well-connected officer, but Mountbatten continued to head Combined Ops and look for unique ways to defeat Germany, confident that science would provide the answers.

Shortly after his appointment as chief of Combined Ops, Mountbatten visited the University of Cambridge to scout out innovators and ideas that might be helpful, or that at least would shake up his conservative organization. There he met Geoffrey Nathaniel Joseph Pyke, a bespectacled and bizarre genius with an endless supply of unconventional and improbable schemes. Pyke also completely disdained established authority, which he described as having the attitude "nothing must ever be done for the first time."

Born in 1893, Pyke was an academic, journalist, educator, inventor and all-round oddball. His father had died when Pyke was five years old, leaving the family destitute. His mother managed to scrape together enough money to send him to an exclusive school primarily for the sons of army officers, but Pyke didn't fit in and was totally miserable. Finally extricated from this establishment, he was tutored privately and admitted to Cambridge in his teens to study law. When the First World War broke out, Pyke left his studies to follow his dream of becoming a war correspondent. Against all odds, he convinced the editor of London's *Daily Chronicle* newspaper that he could be their eyes and ears in Berlin and send back exclusive dispatches about what was happening in the enemy capital. He planned to sample public opinion about current events, especially attitudes about the war. The editor agreed, since he had nothing to lose.

Pyke bought a passport from an American sailor in Amsterdam, travelled north to Denmark and then into Germany. Using his modest German language skills, Pyke talked with civilians he met on the street and observed that life was still pleasant in Berlin. He saw none of the food shortages and hardships that were being reported in the British press. He eavesdropped on conversations in cafés and saw trainloads of soldiers departing to fight the war in the trenches. He was living his dream of being an international spy.

The illusion didn't last long. Pyke's phony documents and snoopy behaviour caught the attention of German authorities, and they started following him almost immediately after his arrival. He was arrested and jailed after six days. Although his guards cheerfully shared the information that he would probably be shot the next morning, days passed without this happening. Alone in his small cell with scant rations, he thought to himself that "the German government was not going to waste four deutschmarks on my keep if it was going to be faced with burial expenses on the fifth day." Pyke missed having writing paper, books and somebody with whom to talk. To amuse himself, he recited the poems of Rudyard Kipling from memory out loud in his dark cell. He petitioned the prison director for permission to whistle. Permission was granted. It occurred to Pyke that perhaps his jailers thought he might be going crazy, but then Pyke discounted the possibility because only a sane man could contemplate insanity. After spending 13 weeks in solitary confinement, he was transferred to another prison, where he was held with other captives and had access to newspapers. He learned that foreigners were quarantined there before being sent to the internment camp at Ruhleben. This, at least, seemed better than being shot at dawn.

Ruhleben was a former racetrack located 6 miles (10 kilometres) west of Berlin. Pyke was given a cot in the stable area, which had been converted into a dormitory for detainees. He finally had human company again and befriended a group of Oxford and Cambridge graduates as they shared warm clothes and whatever food was available, as well as books and games. Occasionally they received parcels from home. Even more infrequently, some money arrived.

In spite of the somewhat improved living conditions, throughout the winter Pyke suffered from pneumonia and food poisoning. He was also obsessed with escaping back to Britain. Other prisoners said it was a lost cause. Some had broken out of the prison, but none had made it out of Germany. Then Pyke met fellow countryman Edward Falk, who also had dreams of permanently departing the premises. Ever the dedicated academic, Pyke interviewed detainees and compiled detailed statistics on previous escape attempts, seeking to discover where they had gone wrong and to find patterns in the failures. He and Falk began a vigorous exercise regime to build up their strength and flexibility. To divert suspicion, they told camp authorities the program had been recommended to them by a fellow prisoner who was a doctor.

An equipment shed in the camp exercise yard was the key to their escape. Every afternoon, the sun was in a position that made it difficult for patrolling guards to see inside the structure, so on June 9, 1915, Pyke and Falk hid inside the shed until dark, then crawled out and climbed over barriers and under wire enclosures. They made it to a spot where trains slowed on their way into Berlin and jumped on the first one that arrived. Once in the city, they bought clothes and train tickets west to the border with the Netherlands. Fearing discovery, they decided it was better to disembark early and go the final distance by foot. The escapees walked in the rain for days, scavenging for food as they waded through muddy ditches, climbed farm fences and hid at every bridge before determining it was safe to cross. Nearing the border, they hid until dusk before navigating the last few steps to freedom. Just as they moved forward, an armed soldier appeared out of nowhere and shouted at them. They froze mid-step. Pyke tried to explain their presence, but after a halting multilingual discussion, they discovered they were already inside neutral Dutch territory—so much for Pyke's orienteering skills. But they had made their escape and returned to Britain via Amsterdam as free men.

Pyke sadly reported to the *Daily Chronicle* editor that he had been a complete failure as a war correspondent. However, the article he wrote about his incarceration and escape was a great success. The British public wanted to read more stories about the adventure, but Pyke was more interested in academic writing. He did, however, produce a memoir of his experiences titled *To Ruhleben—And Back*, the only first-hand description of life in a First World War detention camp. It was published in 1916.

As an escaped prisoner of war, Pyke was exempt from conscription; in addition, he had become a pacifist. In 1918, he met and married Margaret Chubb, who was attracted by his unusual behaviour. Her Prince Charming was a tall man with a goatee, dark-rimmed glasses and a permanently rumpled look. He explained that he wore brightly coloured spats because "they can be worn for weeks and they obviate socks which I'd have to change much more often." To earn money, Pyke speculated in commodities, using his own investment techniques to buy and sell huge stock lots. He explained why he chose a career in finance: "I went into the City and spent a day watching men entering and leaving the Stock Exchange. All of them appeared ineffably stupid, and many of them were my relatives."

When his son David was born in 1921, educational techniques caught Pyke's attention. He wanted a formative training experience for David that was totally different from the one he had endured, one that promoted curiosity and individual development. He proceeded to found Malting House School, which was headed by a psychologist. At the school, students acted as researchers and teachers as observers. Students would follow their curiosity and study only those subjects they found interesting. It was cited as the leading edge of educational reform and was funded by Pyke's investment profits. Unfortunately, since he was providing the operating capital, Pyke believed he should also micromanage the school's daily activities. School staff quit in protest. In 1927, the stock market collapsed, and Pyke lost all his money, his wife and son, his school, his reputation and, quite possibly, his mind. Malting House School closed, and Pyke, facing large debts, battled bouts of depression while living off the charity of friends.

With the outbreak of the Spanish Civil War in 1936, Pyke became interested in the direct implications of conflict, especially the lack of ambulances to transport the wounded to aid stations. He devised a motorcycle prototype to carry medical supplies to battle sites and the injured back for treatment. He raised money to buy big, powerful, used Harley-Davidson motorcycles and convinced unionized machinists to build the sidecars for free. He then had the vehicles shipped to Spain. Not stopping there, Pyke arranged to collect horse-drawn plows no longer used in Britain and send them over to Spanish farmers, along with hand tools for manual labourers. Medical dressings were in short supply, so Pyke recommended sphagnum moss packed into cloth bags as alternative field dressings. Inspired by Pyke, British volunteer collectors soon started sending boxes of moss packets to Spain.

Prior to the outbreak of the Second World War in 1939, Pyke reprised his former information-gathering scheme by setting up an opinion poll with a sports twist. Thinking it would be useful to know what ordinary Germans felt about Adolf Hitler and his Nazi regime, Pyke trained volunteer interviewers himself. The first requirement was that they had to play golf well above the duffer category. They would pose as professional golfers on an international tour that started in Frankfurt and played around the country. Along the way, they would collect valuable intelligence. Against all odds, the project went ahead, and the golf sleuths sent back informative reports. But in late August 1939, responding to warnings from contacts at the British Foreign Office, Pyke quickly recalled his golfers back to London. Britain declared war on Germany on September 3, 1939.

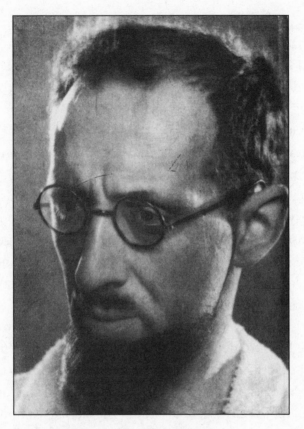

The bizarre genius Geoffrey N. Pyke.
HERALD AND WEEKLY TIMES, STATE LIBRARY OF VICTORIA, AUSTRALIA

Pyke next turned his fertile mind to new ways of winning in modern warfare. He suggested barrage balloons be fitted with microphones so the location of aircraft could be determined by triangulation, completely ignoring that the newly invented RADAR—the acronym for radio detection and ranging—did the same thing. When the war spread to German-held Norway, the joint American-Canadian commando 1st Special Service Force, nicknamed the Devil's Brigade, was originally to parachute into Norway surreptitiously and sabotage vital targets such as key transportation centres and hydroelectric plants. One of these important targets was Rjukan, where the Germans were producing heavy water for their atomic weapons research. Pyke was tasked with discovering ways to transport soldiers quickly over remote snow-covered terrain. He proposed a light, screw-driven track vehicle mounted on cylinders. It would be able to move over the snow, darting in and out of enemy-held positions without the occupying Germans ever knowing where they would be attacked next. He seriously suggested these snow sledges could be hidden until needed in wooden stalls marked (in German) "Officer's Latrine. For Colonels Only" because this would keep all the overly obedient German soldiers from investigating further. Pyke's vehicle design, but without the storage component, was adopted for use and called Operation Plough. The original attack vehicle, called the Weasel, would be built by the Americans, while Canada and the United States would supply the fighting men. The operation never came to pass, but a variation of the vehicle was later used by Allied units in northern Italy and Bavaria.

During their joint work on Operation Plough and the properties of ice and snow, Pyke had taken to lecturing his new American colleagues on the negative effects of capitalism. They thought he was a communist, a security risk or just plain nuts. He preferred to conduct most of his meetings reclining in bed, saying he was too busy to get up and get dressed. He suffered from hypergraphia (incessant writing) and filled endless scrapbooks with notes about his ideas and pasted-in newspaper clippings he considered relevant. (There is no indication he was pagophilic, or ice-loving, in spite of his fascination with frosty weapons of war.) Cigarette butts and empty drink containers littered the floor of his room in the house of an indulgent friend. He existed on a diet of herring and biscuits, his favourite foods. This, along with his scruffy clothing, inattention to personal hygiene and obscure rantings, led the American military men and scientists with whom he worked to believe he was mentally unhinged and needed a rest. They recommended he go to a mental asylum. To their surprise, he readily agreed. Pyke found the institutional environment quiet and restful, which allowed him to spend time dreaming up more outlandish schemes.

Another Pyke brainstorm was to break through and bomb the defences around the Ploieşti Oilfields in Romania, which fuelled the German war machine. The wells would be set on fire by aerial bombardment, then British commando units, dressed as firefighters and riding on fire trucks, would rush in and pretend to extinguish the fires while actually shooting incendiary devices out of their hoses. Alternatively, dogs could be released in the oilfields with barrels of alcohol around their necks, like pseudo–St. Bernards from Switzerland. The guards would drink the alcohol, become intoxicated and be overpowered easily by British soldiers. Or, a team of women could be sent in to "distract" the men guarding the oilfields while solders moved in.

An even more bizarre idea from Pyke was a searchlight that would bring down any aircraft caught in its beam. When a button was pushed, the light beam would solidify. By directing the beam down, the trapped plane would be slammed into the ground. The minor details of how to solidify the beam were, according to Pyke, "merely matters of research and development easily solvable by anyone who really believes in the idea."

But no matter how wild Pyke's ideas were, Mountbatten was pleased and invited him to continue at Combined Ops. In an introductory meeting with Mountbatten, Pyke had declared, "You need me on your staff because I am a man who thinks!" Mountbatten took him at his word, and the two joined forces in a unique synergy based on Pyke's outlandish ideas and Mountbatten's enthusiastic acceptance of them.

2

Big Ideas

LOUIS MOUNTBATTEN WAS AN ENERGETIC, handsome, charming, wealthy and vain polo-playing friend of kings and movie stars. Almost everyone who knew him liked him. His great-grandmother was Queen Victoria, on whose lap he had sat, and the Romanovs of Russia had been his cousins. Ironically, his roots were German; the family name Battenberg was anglicized to Mountbatten in 1917 at the direction of King George V. Edward Prince of Wales, briefly Edward VIII of England before his abdication, was also a cousin and best man at Mountbatten's wedding to the ultra-rich and beautiful Edwina Ashley in 1922. Mountbatten's sisters were Queen Louise of Sweden and Princess Alice of Greece and Denmark. Mountbatten's nephew, the penniless Prince Philip of Greece, married Mountbatten's favourite young cousin, Lilibet, the future Queen Elizabeth II. Mountbatten referred to her as his niece, and after her coronation, aides would bet with each other who would be the first to get him to refer to their relationship. But to the British royal family he was "Dickie," although Richard was not among his string of given names: Louis Francis Albert Victor Nicholas.

In spite of his impressive social and familial connections, Mountbatten was amiable and able to laugh at himself. Ever the optimist, he was reported by his official biographer to have had a "vividly accurate memory for events as they should have happened. Although the truth in his hands often suffered a sea-change, he was genuinely surprised and upset when instances of this were pointed out to him." While not intellectually gifted, he was known by the British establishment to be mentally agile and receptive to the ideas of others. Given these traits, and his royal connections, he rose quickly through the ranks. Dickie Mountbatten was never just another junior officer; he had money by birth and by marriage. While stationed in Malta in the late 1920s, he and his wife kept a 66-ton yacht in the harbour. The writer Noel Coward, actors Douglas Fairbanks and Mary Pickford and an assortment of major and minor royals enjoyed their hospitality.

As a commander of destroyers early in the Second World War, Mountbatten was privileged but rash. His first command was the destroyer HMS *Daring* in 1934, then HMS *Wishart*, followed by the state-of-the-art HMS *Kelly*. By 1939, Mountbatten commanded the 5th Destroyer Flotilla. While rushing to the aid of a tanker that had been mined, *Kelly* suffered the same fate and was badly damaged. She was repaired in dry dock. The next year, she collided with HMS *Mohawk* and was again sent back to dry dock in need of repairs. In 1941, she was sunk off Crete with the loss of over half her crew, but Mountbatten survived. This ended his career as a destroyer commander. It was said, either in admiration or disapproval by commanders of other vessels, that "if a destroyer could leave skid marks, HMS *Kelly* (under Mountbatten's command) would have disfigured every sea in which she sailed."

But there was never any question about Mountbatten's courage, of which he may have had an overabundance. As Field Marshall Bernard Montgomery enjoyed pointing out, Mountbatten had three destroyers sunk under him during the early part of the war and was still successful. His failure at Dieppe in August 1942 was a shock to him as well as to the Allied command and the ordinary citizens who regarded Lord Louis as a favourite near-royal.

Late in 1942, Mountbatten, chief of Combined Ops, paid a visit to Winston Churchill at the prime minister's official country residence, Chequers. It wasn't a social call. Tucked under Mountbatten's arm was a small parcel with big potential. A member of Churchill's staff met Mountbatten

Louis Mountbatten, First Earl Mountbatten of Burma, appeared on the cover of *Maclean's* on February 1, 1944.

YOUSUF KARSH/*MACLEAN'S*, LIBRARY AND ARCHIVES CANADA, PA-215000

the door and apologized that there would be a wait because the prime minister was upstairs taking a bath. Not one to stand on convention when there was a new idea to be put forward, Mountbatten brushed aside the aide and climbed the stairs. Opening the bathroom door, he found the portly prime minister was indeed in the tub and not at all pleased at the interruption. With great flourish, Mountbatten unwrapped his parcel and, despite gruff objections from the tub's occupant, said he had a new substance he was going to drop into the steaming water. With a plop, in went a cube of ice. Both men stared at it as it melted, Churchill still in the tub and Mountbatten standing beside it. The prime minister was not impressed. Then Mountbatten dropped in another small block of ice, which floated on the surface. Minutes went by. Still the ice floated, staying the same size. It had not melted. What was this stuff?

By the spring of 1942, Pyke's active mind had turned from snow vehicles in Norway to giant icebergs floating in the Atlantic. The sinking of *Titanic* in 1912 was only one of 400 known iceberg collisions since 1818, but it had demonstrated just how big and strong icebergs were. So, Pyke reasoned, why not use them to solve the problem of protecting convoys in the Atlantic? He envisioned cutting off immense sections of ice from the Arctic icecap, levelling off the tops and towing them to the war zone to act as aircraft landing platforms. The natural buoyancy of ice would keep the ice ships from sinking in the event of enemy shelling, and the raw material (water) for their repair was essentially free and all around them. However, ice is brittle and tends to creep (deform under pressure), which presents construction difficulties. Alternatively, floating icebergs off

Greenland or Newfoundland could be captured (there were no instructions on how this feat was to be accomplished) and hollowed out so planes, machinery and crew could shelter inside. These giant floating "bergship" aircraft carriers then would patrol the seas. The enemy would be caught off guard, and such a weapon could win the war.

By April 1942, Pyke had been asked by Combined Operations Headquarters (COHQ) to solve the problem of preventing ice buildup on ships patrolling in Arctic waters. He consulted with molecular biologists Professor John Desmond Bernal (called "Sage" by friends) and Austrian chemist Max Perutz, who were working on crystallography and glacier movement in the Cavendish Laboratory at the University of Cambridge. Pyke knew Perutz had also investigated the physical properties of snow with Operation Plough. Leaving the de-icing assignment in good hands, Pyke turned his thoughts back to how ice could be used as a weapon.

In discussing the de-icing work, Perutz had offhandedly commented, "It is not only this country but the whole world which, as compared with knowledge of other natural phenomena, lacks knowledge of snow and ice. This is fortunate, for whoever gets there first may get a great advantage." This got Pyke thinking. Lab staff had already nicknamed him the "Ozzard of Whizz" for his strange requests, but he took no notice. He was concerned with high-level ideas, not with practical how-to details that could be handled by other less imaginative types like engineers and technicians.

With strategic metals in short supply, Pyke realized that ice was an ideal raw material. Being lighter than water, ice would not sink and could be manufactured with only 1 percent of the energy needed to make an equivalent mass of steel. Another advantage was that an ice shell would not attract magnetic mines like a metal hull would. By September 23, 1942, now working in the United States, Pyke had refined his ideas and developed a 35,000-word, 232-page document that outlined many recommendations on how cold could be used to defeat an enemy and how ice could win the war. He proposed many uses for ice and what he called "super-cooled water"— water that had been chilled below freezing (32°F/0°C) but still remained liquid. It could be streamed out of cannon tubes at high pressure onto vehicles and armies to immobilize them immediately, or be used to quickly construct ice roads for tanks and troops. Pyke had no idea how to make super-cooled water, but that was just one of those pesky practical details that kept popping up.

Pyke then moved on to his masterpiece—Habbakuk—immense aircraft carriers constructed from naturally occurring or refrigerated ice. Since regular carriers could only handle small fighter aircraft, these frosty behemoths would be a base for bigger planes and bombers that could protect Atlantic supply convoys. The floating ice vessels could also be landing strips for refuelling on long ocean flights and act as launching pads for amphibious attacks against Europe or Japan.

Odd as it may have sounded, Pyke's idea was among many new weapons technologies suggested by civilian scientists during the Second World War. Others included midget submarines to penetrate harbours, bouncing bombs that skipped over the water to strike a target and then exploded underwater, and the Pipe Lines Under The Ocean (PLUTO) to transport oil from England to France on the floor of the English Channel. In such company, ice aircraft carriers and bergships were not that far out. Many ideas didn't get past the design phase, but others were moved forward and tested before being approved or abandoned.

Pyke's report, wrapped in brown paper and tied with string, had been sent by diplomatic bag in October from New York to London. It included a covering memo to Mountbatten, instructing him to read the first 33-page section before deciding to proceed or not, because, as Pyke had scribbled, "It may be gold; it may only glitter. I can't tell. I have been hammering at it too long and am blinded." And just to catch his patron's eye, Pyke had penned in a quote from G.K. Chesterton, one of Mountbatten's favourite novelists: "It isn't that they can't see the solution. It is that they can't see the problem." This was precisely the approach Lord Louis had been trying to instill into his strategic planners at Combined Ops. Pyke had grasped the concept and used it to advance his "ice will win the war" proposal. Mountbatten read on. Pyke's note urged him not to delegate responsibility for the ice ship but to present it himself to keep it from being buried in the bureaucracy. The note ended with, "The cover name for the project is Habbakuk, *parce qu'il était capable de tout* [because it was capable of anything]."

Mountbatten scanned the first few pages of the document at home, then, in a move that would have disappointed Pyke, he delegated it to his chief of staff, Brigadier Wildman-Lushington. Along with Professor Bernal, Wildman-Lushington thought the main proposals were feasible. The idea to use pure ice was first presented to Churchill as a typewritten recommendation from Combined Ops. On December 4, 1942, Churchill dictated a memo in reply, marked "Most Secret," to his chief of staff, General Hastings Lionel Ismay, enthusiastically supporting the ice-airfields proposal. "I attach the greatest importance to the prompt examination of these ideas," he wrote. "The advantages of a floating island or islands, if only used as refuelling depots for aircraft, are so dazzling that they do not at the moment need to be discussed. There would be no difficulty in finding a place to put such a 'stepping stone' in any of the plans of war now under consideration."

While the prime minister admitted to a limited knowledge of the physical properties of ice, he felt the project could work. He suggested to scientists and engineers that they simply carve the hull of the ship out of Arctic icefields and pour sea water on top of this base to freeze and build it up, much like the process of making a backyard skating rink, only in mammoth proportions. Then, all the necessary equipment would be installed and the colossus towed down to Cornwall near the English Channel. After the planes were added, it would be towed into attack position. Alternatively, floating airfields could be made by cutting the tops off icebergs. The enemy could bomb, strafe and torpedo the icebergs without sinking them. Best of all, ice was free.

Scientific innovations are the result of input from many minds, and Pyke had not been the first to suggest floating mid-ocean landing pads for aircraft, or even to suggest that they could be made of ice. In 1930, German scientific engineer Dr. A. Gerke of Waldenburg conducted some preliminary experiments in Lake Zurich. His proposal for a floating ice station involved the construction of a framework of hollow tubing filled with liquefied air, manufactured in a refrigerating plant, which would freeze the surrounding water into a solid mass suitable for an airport platform. In temperate regions, these ice cakes could be as lasting as rock. On the ocean, two or three ships equipped with refrigeration plants could be anchored at a suitable spot and divers would lay a network of horizontal and vertical pipes into the seabed. As coolant was pumped through these pipes, an island of ice would be created. Once the ice island was formed, a permanent refrigeration unit would keep it frozen. Artificial islands for deeper ocean waters could be formed near shore, towed into position and anchored. Dr. Gerke referred to a situation in 1928 when a sunken ship had been raised from a deep lake in Switzerland by forming a block of ice within the hull to plug a leak.

Churchill directed that research should proceed with the highest priority and that natural freezing should be used as much as possible. He added a prophetic caveat: "The scheme is only possible if we make Nature do nearly all the work for us and use as raw material, sea water and low temperature. The scheme will be destroyed if it involves the movement of very large numbers of men and a heavy tonnage of steel or concrete to the remote recesses of the Arctic night." Under the direction of a central Habbakuk Committee, work began immediately in different locations on the small-scale production of ice and the measurement of its properties.

The British Admiralty calculated that if heavy land-based fighters and bombers were to be flown off a bergship, a runway at least 2,000 feet (610 metres) long and 98 feet (30 metres) wide would be needed. Further investigation revealed that ice cut out of natural ice floes or glaciers would not work because that ice was too thin. Icebergs also proved unsuitable. Because 90 percent of a typical iceberg is under water, the above-water surfaces are small. A useable iceberg would have to be over 500 feet (150 metres) high, and this raised a new set of problems. Icebergs are unstable and prone to rolling over, not a pleasant thought for the navy. The drag created by such a huge mass would make it impossible to manoeuvre in port or in battle. To correct this problem, the iceberg could be hollowed out, but that would make it more vulnerable when attacked—hardly the indestructible vessel they intended. And with a thinner hull, more artificial refrigeration would be needed, plus an insulating outer covering.

Still, the ice-ship concept remained popular in defence circles, mostly because of marine experience in trying to break up iceberg floes and ice jams with explosives. Ice had proven to be a formidable opponent and resistant to attack. After consulting with ice experts and accessing knowledge gained during the First World War about glacier warfare in the Alps, calculations were made showing it was not impossible to construct a large vessel out of ice; it would just be difficult.

On October 6, 1942, Combined Ops drew up a short summary of the objectives of the Habbakuk project in an internal covering document marked "Most Secret." It outlined the use of ice construction for ships of different purposes—from large aircraft carriers to merchant vessels—and maintained that they could be made quickly and cheaply, that they would be practically indestructible by shells, bombs, mines or torpedoes, and that they could be protected from melting even in warm seas by relatively thin insulating material. The document then addressed super-cooled water:

> 2. In addition to this it is proposed to use super-cooled water, transforming spontaneously to ice, for the construction of land fortifications, static and mobile and for the repair of

ice ships. These new methods, which may be summarized as
the use of ice as a strategic material, are to be used to achieve
rapidly certain main strategic aims—

(a) To destroy enemy sea transport by sinking it in port,

(b) To broaden and protect all United Nations sea lanes,
particularly those between the USA, Britain and the USSR,

(c) To force abandonment of the Baltic and Mediterranean seas,

(d) To make landings possible in many parts of enemy
occupied country.

3. The general strategy proposed is that of encouraging the
enemy to exercise the maximum effort at the most distant
points of his field of operations; to immobilise him there
and at the same time cut his lines of communication and
attack his vital centres.

After providing general dimensions and payload capacity, the document went on to describe the basic construction
technique and propose how the ice ships would be employed
to win the war:

It is proposed to make the ship by freezing water on a
gradually built up form-work, by means of a refrigerant
carried through cardboard or plastic pipes. The power
needed is estimated as one ton of Diesel Oil or two tons of
coal per 100 tons of ice made . . .

The large weight of these craft would enable them to
act as Boom Breakers and force their way into any harbour,
given sufficient draft at the entry. For land operations it is

proposed to use super-cooled water for erecting barricades and tank blocks, approximately 20 ft. thick and 15 ft. high, either for protecting towns seized by "coup-de-main" or for besieging towns approached from landings on cliffs. Detailed suggestions are given for attacks on Genoa, Hamburg and the Kiel Canal.

The Royal Navy and the War Office agreed that an ice aircraft carrier would be built to the proposed dimensions of 2,000 by 300 by 200 feet (610 by 90 by 60 metres) gross depth. She would have a displacement of 2,200,000 tons of water, 26 times that of the Cunard Line's RMS *Queen Elizabeth*, the largest ocean-going passenger liner of the time. To keep the proposed ice ship from melting around its cargo and crew, 20 turboelectric motors would be installed to keep it cool. Its propulsion engines would produce 30,000 horsepower, moving it at a top speed of 7 knots (8 miles or 13 kilometres per hour). The proposed carrier would require over 120 tons of diesel fuel a day, so enormous tanks that could hold enough for a 7,000-mile (11,265-kilometre) nonstop journey would be installed. To achieve the best possible results, the ship would be built in Canada or Russia, where winter temperatures were the lowest and natural freezing worked best. The budget for the experimental ship was a measly £5,000, equivalent to approximately £200,000 today. Its construction from an untested material would be a staggering undertaking, but these were desperate times.

Pyke was pleased. Once again he would be working with scientists Bernal and Perutz, whom he now considered colleagues. He knew they had continued their research into the properties of ice, and he had read a paper by researchers Herman Mark and Walter Hohenstein of the Brooklyn Polytechnic Institute's Cold Research Laboratory. They had been involved in Operation Plough and now were working on the American contribution to ice research for the Habbakuk project. They were discovering that ice made from water mixed with wood fibres formed a strong, solid mass that was much stronger than pure ice alone. They experimented with mixtures from 4 to 14 percent wood pulp and found the higher amount worked best. A 4-percent solution produced a porridge-like goop that was quite strong when frozen, but a 14-percent solution had the consistency of wet cement and the strength of concrete when frozen. Pulp worked better than sawdust because the ragged fibres of the pulp created a better interlocking bond than the clean cuts in sawdust. Tests on this composition, which they first called piccolite or pikolite, then simply "pic" and later "pykrete" (Pyke plus concrete), were promising. For the remainder of the project, "pic" was code for ice.

Of course, the secret new material called pykrete that bobbed around in Winston Churchill's bathtub in late December 1942 wasn't really new. Techniques similar to the wood-pulp recipe had evolved long ago in the North. For thousands of years, ice strengthened with tiny pieces of moss and small twigs had been used by Inuit people in the construction of traditional sledges and shelters, but few other cultures had ever seriously considered ice as a structural material until Geoffrey Pyke pursued the idea. Pyke received credit for pykrete, which would later transform the plans for the Habbakuk project, while the contribution of Mark and Hohenstein has been virtually forgotten.

On December 31, 1942, Professor Bernal summed up general conclusions to date about what was referred to as "the material" (ice) in yet another document stamped "Most Secret" for consumption by Combined Ops:

> The known properties of the material and full-scale tests carried out in America have shown—
>
> (a) That the material can be reinforced.
>
> (b) That it is not physically impossible to make a vessel of the material which would stand the stresses it is likely to meet on patrol in the North Atlantic.
>
> (c) If such a vessel were made, it would be unsinkable and it would not suffer any damage which could not be repaired without putting back to port.
>
> (d) That without assisted take-off it would be impossible to use it for fighter aircraft.
>
> Nothing is likely to be found in the next few weeks that should prove the project as a whole unfeasible, but its full feasibility depends on the working out of certain key problems—
>
> (a) The cost and speed of making the material naturally or artificially on a large scale.

(b) The best methods of construction and launching of the vessel.

(c) The cheapness and method of fixing reinforcement.

(d) The most readily available and most reliable thermal insulation.

(e) What kind of engines are required, and how should they be fixed.

(f) Methods of arranging for assisted take-off and arresters.

Bernal went on to write, "there seems good promise that all these problems can be satisfactorily solved if they are given sufficient priority. Second priority will not do." But while small-scale experimental studies were underway in England, full-scale work was needed "which must be undertaken in Canada." Laying out the timetable to make Pyke's futuristic Habbakuk a reality, Bernal continued, "It is essential that the Canadian work should be put in hand now, or the advantages of the weather will be lost for a year, with the result of putting the whole scheme back to 1945. The exploration of the resources of materials, man-power and machinery also must be gone into at this stage."

The research on pykrete assumed an even greater significance when Perutz identified problems with pure ice as a naval construction material. He was discovering that the physical properties of ice make it a curious and unpredictable natural material. He conducted tests to determine how malleable it could be and the extent of physical effects from measured blows. Molded into a beam, it fractures at loads anywhere from 70 to 500 pounds per square inch (5 to 35 kilograms per square centimetre), a wide variation that makes it an unreliable construction material. Ice can snap, fracture and shatter under stress or when hit. Bombs and torpedoes would crack an ice ship, even if they did not sink it. Onboard refrigeration would have to be available to make repairs immediately. And while ice is hard, it is also subject to continuous gravitational pull, which causes glaciers to flow like rivers, faster in the middle than at the sides and faster on the top than on the bottom. Because of this slow flow, creep or "plastic flow," an ice ship would slowly sag and probably break apart under its own weight. The same thing would happen more slowly to a pykrete bergship, unless it was kept cooled to 3.2°F (–16°C). To accomplish this, a bergship's surface would have to be protected by insulation, and it would need a refrigeration plant and a complicated system of ducts to keep it cold enough to stay afloat.

Habbakuk was rapidly escalating from a simple project to a complicated and expensive one. British scientists had submitted a report in January 1943 to the Habbakuk Committee noting that ice is a cheap, natural material but has problems when used in construction. American scientists, they noted, were experimenting with ways to reinforce ice. Mountbatten ordered Pyke to have pykrete produced in larger quantities and further tested in a British laboratory. Utmost secrecy was required, so in February 1943, Pyke, Bernal and Perutz set up shop in the refrigerated meat locker of a butcher's basement at Smithfield Market in London. The area had been a livestock market for over 800 years, plus a wholesale food market for the past 200 years. Now it was a top-secret research laboratory, too. Military commandos were stationed on site dressed as white-coated lab assistants or butcher-shop apprentices—it was never certain which they pretended to be. The investigations into the viability and optimum composition of pykrete were conducted behind a protective screen of massive frozen animal carcasses dangling from ceiling hooks. The researchers tested mechanically ground spruce, pine and other woods, straw, cotton and sawdust but determined that the previously recommended 14 percent dry wood pulp and 86 percent water composition worked best for their bergship purposes. When Mountbatten paid a visit to check on progress, the operation was so hush-hush that Lord Louis had to remove his spiffy naval uniform and dress in "mufti" or civvies, disguising himself as a mere civilian in ordinary clothes.

The Smithfield tests proved the potential of pykrete as a building material. It had a consistent mechanical strength of 996 pounds per square inch (70 kilograms per square centimetre). In one experiment, a 7.69-millimetre rifle bullet fired into pure ice penetrated to a depth of 14 inches (36 centimetres). Fired into pykrete, the bullet penetrated less than half that distance. Yet pykrete could be formed into blocks, machined on a lathe, sawed like real wood and cast into shapes like molten metal. In addition, it had tremendous crush resistance: a 1-inch (2.5-centimetre) thick column of pykrete could balance the weight of "one medium-sized motor car." The tiny fibres of the wood used to make pykrete became imbedded among the ice crystals, keeping surface cracks from deepening into full breaks and eliminating brittleness. The wood fibres also appeared to provide an insulating mesh layer on the surface that kept heat out and cold in.

But while pykrete solved many of the problems encountered with ice and proved to be resilient and environmentally friendly, it brought its own set of issues, such as the additional cost and extra manpower needed to manufacture it. These issues were to loom large as Project Habbakuk pitched and rolled through stormy channels on its way to becoming reality.

CHAPTER

3

Aggressive Icebergs

IN HIS MEMO TO MOUNTBATTEN at the end of September 1942, Geoffrey Pyke christened his masterpiece "Habbakuk," referring to the Book of Habakkuk, the eighth book of the 12 minor prophets of the Old Testament, composed in the late 7th century BC. The prophet Habakkuk complained to God asking why good people must suffer and why cruel people seem to succeed. According to the prophet, the Lord said, "Behold ye among the heathen, and regard, and wonder marvelously: for I will work a work in your days, which ye will not believe, though it be told you." Others contend that the name came from Voltaire's satirical novel *Candide* and was misspelled by Pyke's Canadian secretary, but there is no reference to Habakkuk in that literary work. Whatever the

51

origin, the misspelled version with two b's and two k's, not the biblical one with one b and three k's, held and was used to refer to the project throughout its short lifetime.

The original mammoth carrier was to be approximately the length of six and a half football fields and have a water displacement of 2,000,000 tons, over 50 times the displacement of other aircraft carriers at the time. Habbakuk was to be made from 280,000 blocks of ice. It would carry men, machinery, munitions and have a robust refrigeration system to guarantee it did not fall victim to an even greater enemy than the Germans—heat. This whole frozen fighter concept would fail if the ice ship turned to slush and sailors had to swim for their lives as their ship dissolved around them. On-board armaments were to include 40 dual-barrelled turrets, as well as numerous anti-aircraft guns. The carrier would have the capacity to house up to 150 twin-engine bombers or fighter planes, but it would still look like a floating island, a levelled and cavernous lethal floating chunk of glacial ice—buoyant, unsinkable and easily repaired at sea without ever returning to port.

These massive white hulks would churn through the Atlantic Ocean, launching aircraft, protecting supply convoys and grinding apart the U-boat wolf packs. The Germans would be amazed and terrified. Habbakuk would not be very fast, and the enemy would hardly fail to see it coming, but this was not important. As Pyke said, "surprise can be obtained from permanence as well as suddenness." And Habbakuk would have more than mass and munitions on its side. It would have that super-secret weapon that the lab guys hadn't quite figured out yet. Somehow, coupled with the ship's refrigeration system, there would be icing apparatus that could violently discharge long-range cascades of ultra-cold water to instantly freeze the enemy on contact. Armies and their equipment would be stopped in their tracks. Habbakuk would be Germany's worst nightmare. Most important, it would be cheap to make, so a whole fleet could be assembled quickly. Who wouldn't want a wonder weapon like that?

It had certainly caught Winston Churchill's imagination. He described it as being "of ship-like construction, displacing a million tons, self-propelled at low speed, with its own anti-aircraft defence, with workshops and repair facilities, and a surprisingly small refrigerating plant for preserving its own existence." As plans for the great ship evolved, it soon became apparent that the requirement for a 50-foot (15-metre) freeboard, denoting the depth to which a vessel may be loaded for waters in which it is operating, could only be achieved with a significantly hollowed-out vessel. Solid ice, pure or reinforced, would have required too deep a draft, in the range of 150 feet (45 metres). And construction using new, untried materials was a daunting task. On the naval drawing board, for the sake of simplicity, the ship was shaped like a hollow rectangular beam with bevelled edges to reduce drag and help it slip through the water. After seeing the outline, one draftsman labelled it the "ice lozenge." Designers envisaged the outside walls of each ship wrapped in 40,000 tons of cork insulation. Thousands of miles of steel tubing for circulating the brine coolant would both freeze and reinforce the hull.

A secret Combined Ops briefing note, dated January 8, 1943, and titled *Habbakuk: Notes on Practicability of Scheme*, described the project's advantages and disadvantages:

1. Costless fabrication of material [ice] compared with fuel and labour for other material in equivalent quantities.

2. Gravity placing of the material with the minimum use of labour . . . The material would never be lifted at any stage, it would slide down into place under its own weight. The labour required for this is almost certainly over-estimated at 10,000 per ship; half this figure is quite likely.

3. Self welding. Joining blocks of the material, say of 100 tons weight, can be effected simply by letting them stick together with a little water between.

4. Build very large vessels in a time no more than a tenth or a twentieth of that which it would take to build them by fabrication in the ordinary ways . . . that a vessel should be available in 1944.

Two major disadvantages are—
1. Lack of knowledge as to mechanical strength and reliability. The material is known to be plastic and brittle, but it should be possible to overcome these disadvantages by suitable design.

> 2. The need for insulant and permanent insulation. The outstanding problem . . . is to find a suitable cheap insulant which will stick well to ice.

In conclusion, the document stated, this was a war emergency job, and therefore it was worth running some big risks to bring it off. Even if the proposed bergship lacked exceptional performance in mid-Atlantic storms or was not fully capable of withstanding concentrated enemy attack, and one or more were put out of action, such a fate inevitably happened to the best of His Majesty's Ships on the high seas. The advantage of using the bergships in action would well outweigh any lost effort. For this reason, the normal procedure of elaborate testing prior to launch could well be waived in the current situation. The main value of the bergship scheme lay in its ability to provide an early solution to a persistent problem and to accomplish this objective it was worth pushing forward either full out or not at all. In short, Habbakuk was on the fast track to becoming reality.

Initial testing was ramped up and dispersed among multiple university and military laboratories in the United Kingdom and the United States. Tests were replicated that proved and reproved the findings that reinforced ice was more resistant to projectiles and explosives than pure ice. Pykrete was weight for weight as good as concrete. A bullet would cause only insignificant damage: a crater 1 inch (2.5 centimetres) wide and .05 inches (1.2 centimetres) deep.

From the results of underwater explosive tests, it was calculated that a torpedo hit would produce a crater 10 feet (3.0 metres) in diameter and 20 inches (60 centimetres) deep. With a top speed of about 7 knots (8 miles or 13 kilometres per hour), pykrete aircraft carriers would be slow, but since their thick walls would be impervious to bombs and torpedoes, acceleration and agility were not necessary. They could simply shove their way through any situation.

Although pykrete was mechanically strong, like pure ice it would slowly deform under constant pressure, and since the bergship would be hollow, its walls could creep inwards unless they were reinforced by some kind of internal skeleton. And a crack could still theoretically cause the whole structure to flood. However, an ocean of raw repair material would be close at hand. Chunks could be chipped off a nearby iceberg and used to plug leaky spaces, water could be frozen to make emergency repairs, and even though they weren't glaciologists, average sailors could still throw in some wood pulp for reinforcement. The proponents of bergships would not be discouraged from following their dream.

Experiments were undertaken to retest different types of wood pulp to determine how well they reinforced pure ice. Canadian spruce performed better than Scotch pine.

With spruce pulp, creep would stop after an initial period of sagging over a few weeks, but only if the pykrete temperature was kept below 5°F (−15°C). The ship's design

A perspective drawing of *Habbakuk*, the giant ice ship proposed by Geoffrey Pyke, director of programs at COHQ. NATIONAL FILM BOARD OF CANADA. PHOTOTHÈQUE/LIBRARY AND ARCHIVES CANADA PA-171611

was altered to include refrigeration plants that circulated compressed air at −22°F (−30°C) through a network of ducts.

Although it was still being referred to as a bergship, the vessel was starting to bear little resemblance to an iceberg. The bureaucrats and planners were adding new specifications and embellishments that took little heed of Churchill's admonition to "make Nature do nearly all the work." At one design meeting, it was decided the entire hull, as well as the flight deck, was to be sheathed in timber. Below that layer would be the cooling system, insulation and finally ice. The issue of speed was brought up again. Yes, Habbakuk was slow and could not outrun enemy ships, but she was resistant to attack, and even a torpedo would leave only a small "bruise" of about three feet (one metre) on her hull. Her natural floating ability would remain intact, and the cooling system would seal up any damage by immediately reforming ice in the affected area.

Another issue for discussion was the enormous crew needed for such a vessel. It was decided that Habbakuk's crew was to consist of 334 officers, 40 warrant officers, 164 chief petty officers and over 1,052 enlisted crewmen. After all, housed on her two decks of hangars would be 200 Spitfire and 100 Mosquito combat aircraft. To reduce material costs for steel, pykrete ramps would be used to transport aircraft to and from the flight deck, rather than conventional lifts. Then there was the problem of how to keep the crew warm inside a ship of ice that had to be kept cold. Should they be issued snowsuits, or should the crew quarters have extra insulation to keep the cold out?

Project designers who had been directed to build Habbakuk out of blocks of ice soon realized, even before lab tests came in, that it would be nearly impossible to build a carrier of the required dimensions solely out of ice. The insurmountable task of cutting out pieces of an iceberg or a glacier large enough to use in the project perplexed scientists, as did the known problems of low tensile strength and breaking point. They conducted endless laboratory tests on the "modus of rupture." Beams of many different materials were supported at both ends and targeted pressure applied in the middle until they broke. Even a beam made out of a light wood like pine proved much stronger than an ice beam. It was now obvious that while ice was plentiful and resisted ocean liners like *Titanic* very well, it did not fare well against sharp projectiles. Pykrete would be an essential component in any ice ship.

Naval architects continued to refine Habbakuk's specifications. Now it had to have a range of over 7,000 miles (11,200 kilometres) and withstand the largest waves ever recorded. The Admiralty had more requirements. She had to be not just torpedo-resistant, but torpedo-proof, so the hull needed to be at least 40 feet (12 metres) thick, if not more. The Fleet Air Arm decided that heavy bombers should be able to take off from her deck, so that meant it would have to be extended. And the ship's steering needed to be refined. The Royal Navy decided a stern rudder was essential after all, even though it was initially agreed that the ship could be steered by varying the speed of the motors on either side of the hull. A wooden rudder would not be strong enough, and strategic metals like steel were in short supply. Mounting and controlling a rudder 100 feet (30 metres) high was a monumental problem. In fact, the whole project was becoming a monumental problem.

4

The Canadian Prototype

ALTHOUGH THE ICE-SHIP IDEA originated in England, Canada was assigned the responsibility of conducting definitive tests on the practicality and usefulness of using ice as a ship-building material. After all, when you thought of ice, cold, frozen Canada came immediately to mind. One-third of Canada's land mass lies above the Arctic Circle. And it was part of the dear old British Empire. In early 1943, the Admiralty approached the Canadian government to solicit their assistance. Prime Minister Churchill sent a personal request to Prime Minister Mackenzie King. As part of the joint war effort, would they conduct a feasibility project that would research the construction parameters and costs of an ice vessel? Research could be done in various locations across Canada because the cold northern temperatures provided much longer working periods throughout the year.

In January 1943, the Canadian government officially agreed to undertake feasibility research, construction of a ship and the related costs. The National Research Council of Canada (NRC), under acting president Dr. C.J. Mackenzie, was tasked with the building and testing of a scale model. Mackenzie, born at St. Stephen, New Brunswick, in 1888, had been trained in civil engineering at Dalhousie and Harvard universities and served during the First World War before moving west and becoming dean of engineering at the University of Saskatchewan. From there, he moved to the NRC in Ottawa in 1939, hand-picked to succeed NRC president Andrew McNaughton, who had been appointed inspector general of the First Canadian Infantry Division and posted overseas.

Mackenzie was McNaughton's personal choice to replace him while he was on military duty, but he had to champion his appointment before a doubtful Prime Minister Mackenzie King, the staunch Liberal Party leader. At a meeting on Parliament Hill to discuss who would lead the NRC in its wartime scientific support role, McNaughton said he intended to appoint Jack Mackenzie. The prime minister was shocked and blurted out, "But he's another Conservative!"

"Does it really matter?" McNaughton asked.

After a long silence, Mackenzie King replied, "No,

I guess not." As with McNaughton's appointment, the capability of the person triumphed over petty politics. So "Dean" C.J. Mackenzie became the federal government's chief scientist during the Second World War, the right-hand man of C.D. Howe, minister of munitions and supply, and then played a key role in drafting Canada's post-war science policy, including atomic energy. As acting president of the NRC from 1939 to 1943, while General McNaughton, still technically the president, was on leave of absence commanding Canada's field forces, Mackenzie exchanged a series of secret letters with the general, keeping him appraised of ongoing pure research and technological progress in the NRC's laboratories, while receiving in return letters about what was happening in London.

In his diary, Prime Minister Mackenzie King referred to the Habbakuk ice fortress assignment as "another of those mad, wild schemes [that started] with a couple of crazy men in England." C.J. Mackenzie also had reservations, writing in his diary, "I am quite sure that if it were suggested in normal circles here we should not have the ghost of a chance of getting it before even a minor official." But that was not important—his job now was to get moving and get results. At a meeting with his security-cleared staff and private-sector contractors in Ottawa, Mackenzie tabled a 100-page report sent over from London on how to "cut the pattern of an ice ship out on the surrounding surface." The initial reaction was disbelief. The British were bonkers! The navy must

Chalmers Jack (C.J.) Mackenzie was president of the National Research Council of Canada from 1944 to 1953 and directed the Canadian research on Habbakuk. NATIONAL RESEARCH COUNCIL OF CANADA

have frozen some of their own brain cells in coming up with this idea. However, the meeting finally settled down, and the discussion turned to ways of making this fantasy of a floating ice airfield a reality that could be "constructed, protected or even operated." The decision was made to build an outdoor prototype to examine insulation and refrigeration techniques and to test how it would withstand artillery fire and explosives while other tests proceeded at laboratories.

Canadian engineers, naval architects, designers and NRC scientists were sucked into the vortex of Project Habbakuk. The pulp and paper industry was brought in too because it quickly became obvious that pure ice was not practical. While laboratories in the United States and England were carrying out research on pykrete, other recipes would be tried in the NRC and university labs. Sawdust, wood chips, twigs, recycled paper, straw, hemp, cotton, jute, flax, hardwood and softwood—the hunt was on for plants that would reinforce ice the way rebar reinforced concrete. All possible components were to be tested, along with mechanical and chemical pulping processes to grind them and freeze them in water. And instead of being carved from nature, ice would have to be manually formed into blocks or slabs and Mother Nature given a helping hand with electrical refrigeration units. No human being would be able to work outside for the months it would take to hack a ship out of glacial ice or ice floes in the sub-zero temperatures of the Arctic Archipelago. Canadians were a resilient bunch, but there were limits. The NRC received a paltry $50,000 government grant to quickly study all aspects of constructing the Habbakuk ice ships.

By the end of January 1943, Mackenzie had research studies on the properties of ice underway at the universities of Manitoba, Saskatchewan and Alberta, as well as at two labs in Ottawa and one in Montreal. They were investigating methods of joining blocks of frozen materials, reinforcing them and testing their tensile strength. Large-scale outdoor ice tests were to be conducted at two yet-to-be-chosen remote sites out west. Mackenzie decided it was more important at this early stage to determine the practical difficulties of construction than to obtain complete and detailed scientific results. Laboratories in New York and London were kept in the ice-study information loop.

But where to build the real Habbakuk? The Pacific coast of North America was quickly considered and rejected—Alaska was too remote and Puget Sound, in the state of Washington, was too warm. Siberia and the Arctic coast of northern Russia (then part of the Union of Soviet Socialist Republics, shortened to the USSR) certainly had some of the coldest temperatures on the planet, but the population was sparse and there were few supply routes. In addition, Winston Churchill was becoming suspicious of the political motives of the Western Allies' comrade-of-convenience, Joseph Stalin. Sept-Îles, Quebec, and Corner Brook, Newfoundland, were also considered as possible construction sites for building the full-size Habbakuk. Both were near large pulp mills and had cold winters and deep ports. Construction along the Saguenay River was also a possibility but was quickly rejected because of the river's shallowness near its mouth with the St. Lawrence River. The credibility of the project and of Canada's part in it would be permanently damaged if the biggest ship in the world got stuck on a sandbar like a beached whale. Churchill, Manitoba, was also a candidate, but its severe cold was judged too extreme for men to work long hours outdoors, even on a project that required cold temperatures.

Because of its deep harbour and direct Atlantic Ocean access, Corner Brook was chosen as the best construction site. But it was not without problems: it had a small population and an inadequate supply of local workers, the harbour was iced in from mid-December to the end of April, and while its east-coast maritime winters were long, they were not necessarily cold enough for the fast, hard freeze needed for bergship building. Finally, during the Second World War, the Dominion of Newfoundland was still outside the Dominion of Canada. Initially a British colony, it had been granted self-government from 1907 to 1934, then ruled by a joint commission of the Dominions Office in London until 1949, when it joined Canada as the tenth province. This convoluted jurisdictional maze could cause administrative problems when wartime decisions had to be made and implemented quickly without the niceties of multi-level diplomatic consultation.

Design work, Mackenzie decided, would be centred in Ottawa and Montreal, while two remote sites in Rocky Mountain national parks were chosen as the outdoor demonstration sites. Patricia Lake near Jasper, Alberta, would

Secluded Patricia Lake, in Jasper National Park, was chosen as the site for the top-secret military project that tested ice as a ship-building material. NATIONAL RESEARCH COUNCIL OF CANADA

be where the 1:50 scale model would be built to test ice construction and refrigeration processes. It was a strange place to build a seagoing vessel, but the location had advantages for a secret project. No spy would think to look there for a British Admiralty nautical undertaking, and work could proceed without public interference because of the small resident population and distance from big cities. Lake Louise (named after Queen Victoria's fourth daughter) was colder, but Patricia Lake (named for one of Queen Victoria's granddaughters) was a more remote and secure location, while still having good rail access and a ready source of workers from the nearby camp for conscientious objectors. An electric generating station at Jasper Park Lodge, which was closed for the season, could be readily tapped to provide power. An added bonus was the area already had restricted public access because ski paratroopers were training in the surrounding mountains before being deployed as winter warriors for potential cold-weather combat in Bavaria and northern Italy. In rough terrain with no roads, soldiers on skis had a distinct advantage. Few people, it was hoped, would notice additional government and military activity in this secluded Alberta region.

Studies of natural lake ice started in January 1943, and Beverly Evans, seconded from Canadian Industries Limited in Montreal, was the man assigned to handle that part of the research. He arrived at Lake Louise by mid-February to set up an ice-beam testing site right on the lake. Just before his arrival, the closed road from Banff had to be cleared of 4- to 8-foot (1.2- to 2.5-metre) snowdrifts. It was a lengthy process, and after a narrow passage was plowed, much manual labour still remained to be done. The scientists and workers had to dig out Deer Lodge, the facility contracted to accommodate and feed on-site personnel. Food was brought in, and the lodge was heated, since it was normally shut for the winter months. Next they had to tap into the Canadian Pacific Railway power penstock to get a winter water supply for the lodge. Roads still had to be plowed from Deer Lodge to the site selected for the work, which was on the north shore of Lake Louise about a quarter mile (.04 kilometres) west of the Chateau Lake Louise. The hotel was closed to the public during the Second World War because of economic and travel restrictions, including gas rationing. Next, a tractor fell through the ice while clearing an area for the workers to set up.

Before one ice crystal could be tested, wood to make the forms for ice beams had to be hauled 8 miles (12.8 kilometres) from the sawmill site. Then the lumber had to be cut and nailed into the required sizes. Traffic barriers and "Restricted Area" signs were posted on the road leading to the lodge during the work period. No unauthorized person who strayed into the vicinity, whether by accident or due to curiosity, was allowed entry. Identification was always checked, but everybody knew each other, so a strange face would have been immediately noticed. Near the end of the project in March, when spring was in the air and the temperatures were not cold enough to make ice quickly, much work had to be done at night under artificial light.

Aside from these minor inconveniences, the work went well. The major task was to construct and stress-test 30 large, reinforced ice beams from 11 to 40 feet (3.4 to 12.2 metres) in length. They were made by freezing various mixtures of snow or chipped ice in water, or freezing together ice slabs cut from the lake with fresh water drawn from holes cut through the lake ice. Next, seven experiments were conducted to discover the effect of explosives on the ice cover of the lake. For six of them, dynamite was placed under the ice, and for the seventh, a detonator was exploded in an air bubble inside a 4-foot (1.25-metre) block of ice. As the testing progressed, Mackenzie received regular reports from all the inside and outside work sites, contributing his own expertise and emphasizing that negative results and unresolved problems were just as useful in the search for knowledge as successes. One of the greatest contributions made by the Canadian program to the ice-ship project was this large-scale testing to identify the practical difficulties of coping with fluctuating temperature conditions. Such conditions were exactly what a ship would undergo when at sea. The work at Lake Louise indicated that an ice hull at least 35 feet (11 metres) thick would be needed to contain damage from exploding bombs and torpedoes.

In spite of supervising all this activity, Mackenzie found the time and self-discipline to continue writing regular and detailed correspondence about "the mission from England" to General McNaughton, in addition to dictating his daily diary. Mackenzie's tenure at NRC oversaw a tenfold expansion of the institution from 300 to 3,000 staff and scientists, plus top-secret gas, aviation, radar and atomic bomb research, membership on the US-British-Canadian

Workers cut ice and form it into beams for research on Lake Louise near the Chateau Lake Louise resort hotel. NATIONAL FILM BOARD OF CANADA. PHOTOTHÈQUE/LIBRARY AND ARCHIVES CANADA PA-171609

Combined Policy Committee, allocation of uranium supplies, and even the honour of telling Winston Churchill about Habbakuk test results. Since the project was a collaboration among the British government and its scientists, the National Parks Branch (of the Department of the Interior), the universities of Alberta, Saskatchewan and Manitoba, and NRC staff, they all had to work together to complete testing and compile results before spring breakup in 1943.

If a full-size Habbakuk was to help in the war effort to close the Atlantic Gap against U-boat attacks, construction needed to move forward quickly so it would be afloat by

1944. Fieldwork progressed at all the various sites with most of the design work for an ice model done at the NRC labs in Ottawa and the Montreal Engineering Company in Montreal. As the British, American and Canadian scientists were investigating the challenges of ice-ship design and the properties of its frozen construction material, work continued on ways to strengthen both.

For once, Geoffrey Pyke had no whimsical suggestions about strange ingredients that would make ice stronger, but he was very anxious to see how things were going in Canada. In February 1943, he was given the go-ahead to leave London and come to Canada to see how his new strategic project was progressing. Mountbatten sent a letter to Malcolm MacDonald, High Commissioner for Canada, giving him a heads-up:

> [Pyke was] forwarding a new strategic project of his, Habbakuk, on which, quite literally, the length of the war turns. The Prime Minister has been in a white heat of ferocious enthusiasm ever since he learned of it. I do not need to refer to him again, but assure you that he wants everything that can be, to be done to further Habbakuk. I should tell you, in the strictest secrecy, that the PM told the President of the project immediately on landing at Casablanca. The President's enthusiasm now equals the PM's. However, it is now the quality and weight of the effort that the Canadian Government is able to put behind their part in the matter that success now turns. It is inevitable, as

well as desirable, that they play the major part. As official request for support was made to them by the War Cabinet, and from such news as we have they seem to have responded nobly. But in the time available they have a gigantic task in front of them, requiring not only the greatest energy, but vision . . . Pyke who is Programmes Advisor here, will be joined by a remarkable man, my Senior Scientific Advisor, Professor J. D. Bernal.

When C.J. Mackenzie was told he would he receiving visitors, he replied that they would be welcome, but their arrival was probably too late for them to have much impact on the Canadian program, which had been underway for some weeks. His team already included skilled scientists and engineers with large-scale construction experience, and they were fully engaged in both lab and fieldwork. What more could Pyke add?

In late February, Pyke was in New York reviewing the work of Dr. Mark and Professor Hohenstein in further developing reinforced ice materials. He and Mackenzie had an introductory meeting there before Pyke arrived in Canada on March 1. Mackenzie found Pyke strange, to say the least, and was less than impressed with his behaviour, saying he ignored military and social norms and irritated colleagues unnecessarily. His ideas were fanciful, difficult and often impossible to transform into reality. Mackenzie was aware Pyke had been removed from Operation Plough because people could not work with him. Now he fully understood why. Bernal, however, was a well-respected physicist and acknowledged expert on explosives and research on the effect of bombs. Mackenzie thought he could work with him on a professional basis.

After briefings in Ottawa, Mackenzie escorted Pyke and Bernal by train to visit the work sites in western Canada. It was a memorable trip. Neither Pyke nor Bernal owned watches. Mackenzie noticed that Bernal had no sense of time, and Pyke "didn't care a damn." Travelling with Pyke was like babysitting a rambunctious child. If you took your eyes off him, he disappeared, and you never knew where he had gone or if he would reappear in time to catch the connecting train. At the Ottawa train station, they could not find their luggage. Pyke went to look for it. Bernal went to look for Pyke. Mackenzie corralled both of them, and when they got to their train car the luggage was there waiting for them. Mackenzie breathed a sigh of relief and settled in for the journey. They stopped at Winnipeg, where the bond strength between ice and wood or steel was being studied at the University of Manitoba, then on to Saskatoon on March 4, where work on ice-compression testing and plasticity was going well at the rented cold-storage plant and the University of Saskatchewan.

Sometime during the trip—he had no idea where— Pyke lost his ticket for the ride from Edmonton to Jasper. Mackenzie had to buy him another ticket using his own money. However, research being undertaken in Edmonton on bond and tensile strength was encouraging, and the 1:50 scale model on Patricia Lake was progressing with the first layer of ice blocks laid down and the cold-air ducts ready for positioning. At Lake Louise on March 8, the trio observed large-scale beam tests and dynamite explosions under the lake ice. They discussed the paradoxical brittle yet ductile behaviour of ice. Everything seemed to be going well. They were to leave by train the next day and return to Ottawa. To fill in some free time, Pyke and Bernal decided to go skiing on the nearby glacier. Of course, neither man had a watch. Bernal returned around noon, and Pyke just made it for the late-afternoon train, offering no explanation and no apology. Mackenzie wrote about Pyke in his diary:

> He never does anything because other people do it. He lands in this country without any gloves and with only a light raincoat to embark upon a trip into the Arctic weather. When we were in the mountains he went skiing in the most grotesque outfit—a little hat on the top of his head with his muffler and raincoat and a pair of spats . . . Altogether he is a most unusual type and most people think he is absolutely mad. He is not mad. He thinks in a most unorthodox way . . . He has moments of what amounts to intellectual intoxication when he is seized with his ideas.

Bernal reported back to Combined Ops in London that the work already done in Canada combined with ice-reinforcement data from the American and English labs "had not brought to light any insuperable or unexpected difficulty in constructing the vessel." His overly optimistic report did not fully appreciate the more conservative position developing in Canada about the feasibility of building a full-size Habbakuk. In British military circles, it was assumed that the first bergship would be completed and launched to do battle in the mid-Atlantic by the spring of 1944.

5

The Boathouse
on the Lake

MUCH OF THE MANUAL LABOUR of building the prototype on Patricia Lake was assigned to conscientious objectors (COs), men who on the grounds of freedom of thought, religion or conscience took a stand for non-violence and refused active combat or military service during the Second World War. Canadian COs were given the choice of non-combat service, such as working in the medical or dental corps, or working in institutions, parks and on infrastructure improvements under civilian supervision. Over 95 percent chose the latter and were placed in alternative-service camps by the government for the length of the fighting overseas. They worked in agriculture, education and hospitals, battled forest fires, planted trees, cleared brush and repaired roads or trails. Some were taken to camps in Canada's national parks, where they lived in bunkhouses and worked under the supervision of park staff. Nearly all of the primarily fundamentalist Christian, Mennonite, Hutterite and Doukhobor COs during the Second World War cited personal religious motivations for not joining the military and fighting. One CO said he had wanted to serve on the battlefield as a humanitarian member of the Red Cross, but the military insisted that to do so he had to carry a gun. His Mennonite upbringing forbade taking up arms, so he declined and was sent to work at Patricia Lake.

To the general Canadian population, COs were considered cowards or leeches who chose to live off the ultimate sacrifice of others. Most COs came from the provinces of Manitoba (3,021), Ontario (2,636), Saskatchewan (2,304), British Columbia (1,665) and Alberta (1,184). During the Second World War, nearly 750,000 men applied for a postponement of military service. Some were given temporary delays, but 262,634 had their service "postponed" for the entire length of the war. Of these, only 4 percent (10,782) were COs. Most of the other 96 percent were termed essential workers, like farmers, miners, loggers and factory workers whose regular jobs provided Canada with food to eat, coal for factory furnaces, metals for machinery, wood for houses and other essential consumer goods and war provisions.

In 1941, CO camps were established in Banff (143 men), Kootenay (124 men), Jasper (72 men), Riding Mountain (48 men) and Prince Albert (20 men) national parks. Some

860 men worked at rural camps in other locations. Their primary task was the prevention and suppression of forest fires and the control of insect infestations. Crews improved tourist facilities and built fire roads and trails, fences, dams, bridges, culverts and telephone lines through the wilderness. The COs worked a 48-hour week and were paid monthly. They could not leave camp or have visitors without written permission from the camp foreman; they were not allowed to possess firearms or alcohol, and they had to be in bed by 10:30 p.m., when the lights were turned out.

It was 15 of these conscientious objectors at Jasper, sent from the National Parks Bureau of the Canadian Department of Mines and Resources, who were given the task of building the Habbakuk prototype under the supervision of NRC scientists. Because it looked more like a large barn than a ship, the workers were unaware initially of the exact purpose of the structure they were building. In a letter to Rev. David Toews, Rev. John Wiebe writes, "On the ice of Lake Patricia they are building a box 60 x 30 and 20 feet high, which is to be filled with ice and then sunk. Since spring is approaching, they are rushing to be finished with the work on the ice and thus are working day and night in two 11 hour shifts."

When some of the men found out their alternative-service work was in aid of creating the world's biggest wartime aircraft carrier—a massive ship that would hunt in the seas like a glacial avenger obliterating all opposition—they sat down and refused to pick up their tools. They were quickly moved off site, replacements were moved in, and work continued without a hitch.

Bernal had informed COHQ that the Canadians were building a 1,000-ton prototype, and it was expected to take eight men two weeks to complete the job. Mountbatten responded that Churchill had invited the Chiefs of Staff Committee to have an order placed at once for one complete ship. Further ships would be ordered immediately if it appeared the fighting ice-airbase project was certain of success.

The physical work at Jasper National Park was supervised by Major J.A. Wood, park superintendent. Scientific advice was provided by on-site NRC scientist Dr. C.D. Niven. The objective was not so much to build an exact replica of a ship but rather to construct a large refrigerated and insulated block of ice that would float. This outdoor work would study the two paradoxical elements of unmodified (crystalline) ice: plastic flow and brittleness. Pykrete tests would continue in laboratories. The national park building project would provide practical information on the problems of fabricating a large structure from ice blocks and on thermal performance during and after construction.

Initially, it had been planned to assemble the structure on Lac Beauvert, near the town of Jasper, but because of warm weather that winter the work site was relocated to Patricia Lake, which was 500 feet (150 metres) higher in elevation but still had good access to trains and supplies. However, Major Wood pointed out in a report on the period February 1 to March 31, 1943, that six weeks of freezing temperatures were required to bring the ice-building project to a successful conclusion, and a review of annual temperatures for Jasper over the preceding years would have made it apparent that this was unlikely. He went on to say that had the project been scheduled six weeks earlier, sufficiently cold weather would have been guaranteed.

Soon after work got underway on Patricia Lake, it was suggested that the project be moved once again; however, the decision to remain near Jasper was correct, according to Wood, because a "move to some other location in the Dominion" would have been a waste "so great we would have gained nothing." He also pointed out that due to the inexperienced workforce of COs employed on the project, especially in operating mixers and placing the insulating material, the first pours were anything but successful. Many of the men were not accustomed to all-day outdoor physical labour, especially in the winter, and few had experience in the trades. Skills in carpentry, bricklaying, machining or sheet metal work were either not available in the CO contingent assigned to the project or were withheld as a form of passive resistance.

Scale-model construction got off to a late start on the frozen lake surface. The slow arrival of necessary supplies by rail delayed the beginning of work on the construction challenges and thermal behaviour of ice. In the interim, workers were kept busy with experiments on ways to bond blocks of ice cut from the lake. As this continued, one work crew cleared snow from a large area while another laid the wood floor on top of the frozen lake and framed the walls with 3-by-6-inch (7.6-by-15.2-centimetre) studs and 3-by-8-inch (7.6-by-20.3-centimetre) floor joists. The wood floor and walls were then prepared for insulation and covered with asphalt. Tinsmiths began fitting the ducts inside the structure. Between March 1 and 6, the first layer of ice blocks cut from the lake was placed over the floorboards.

But then came the discovery that the long train ride to the site had damaged the joints of the piping, letting the brine coolant leak out. As a result, it was decided to use cold forced air instead. Three Freon compressors would distribute the cold air throughout the ice by a network of 6-inch (15.2-centimetre) galvanized metal cooling pipes. Such problems had to be solved on the fly to meet calendar and weather deadlines. They also led scientists and engineers overseeing the project to begin to have doubts about the whole scheme.

By March 20, the piping along the floor, the air ducts and all of the wall piping were installed. As more and more ice was placed inside the structure, the floor began to buckle underneath the weight. To relieve some of the strain on the floor, and to test the structure's ability to float in water—

The base for the ice-ship prototype was constructed on the frozen surface of Patricia Lake in Jasper National Park.

NATIONAL RESEARCH COUNCIL OF CANADA

which was, after all, a basic requirement—lake ice was cut out from underneath the structure and it was freed from its solid support. To the great relief of scientists, the ice barge sank to the level of the ice flooring inside, but the entire structure remained afloat.

Crews continued to work on the structure as it floated in frigid Patricia Lake. By the next week, a third layer of ice blocks had been laid and a deep channel cut across the surface. This channel provided a conduit over which the refrigeration unit would sit. After installing more ductwork, the remaining space in the structure was filled with ice. Sawdust was put down over the ice before a hot insulating mixture of asphalt and charcoal was poured and then vermiculite spread on top. But when everything was supposed to be finished, the prototype developed a serious leak in one corner. Ice and insulating materials had to be removed, repairs made and the entire structure sealed up again. By now, the lake ice was starting to melt, so the ice house was held in place by an anchoring system provided by the navy. Construction continued until April 10, when the remaining machinery for the refrigeration unit was installed.

To cap it off, a roof was built over the entire structure to protect the machinery and insulation from the outside elements and from curious eyes or "enemy reconnaissance" from above. The sloping roof, similar to those found on cottage boathouses, gave the scale model its first nickname: the boathouse. The finished dimensions of the boathouse, totally covered by wood, were exactly the specified 60 by 30 by 20 feet (18 by 9 by 6 metres). It weighed 1,000 tons and had a one-horsepower engine to run the refrigeration unit and the system of pipes circulating cold air, as per the specifications received from England. It was not so much a ship as a perpetual ice block—and it had been built by a handful of men in just two months. The objective had been to identify—and perhaps solve—the problems of building a large

The ice-ship prototype under construction at Patricia Lake is inspected by NRC scientists and local builders. NATIONAL RESEARCH COUNCIL OF CANADA

ice (not pykrete) structure from blocks and assess its ongoing thermal performance. Mission accomplished. The ice ship in the Rockies survived through a hot summer without attracting attention, although it was described as looking like a floating chicken coop out in the water. One of the conscientious objectors recalled that during construction the crew referred to it as Noah's Ark.

As the completion date for the prototype approached, a security scare hit the Patricia Lake site. It appeared the true

Conscientious objectors and scientific staff worked together to frame the walls that would support ice blocks and refrigeration ducts of the ice-ship prototype on Patricia Lake.

NATIONAL RESEARCH COUNCIL OF CANADA

purpose of their work deep in the Rocky Mountains had been discovered. An episode of the newspaper cartoon strip *Superman* contained references to iceberg ships. The storyline was that somewhere in the Arctic a group called the Hooded Men used a laser gun to cut away icebergs. (Certainly Churchill would have been glad of their help to "carve out the hull of a ship" for his original Habbakuk concept.) But these were no ordinary icebergs; they had engines and enough explosive material to blow a ship to smithereens. They also had strong electromagnets that would cause the icebergs to go to a ship "like a homing pigeon." The particular ship in question was *Gigantic*, the first atomic passenger liner, which was carrying top-secret cargo and had Clark Kent and Lois Lane on board.

The liner and the icebergs were on a collision course when Superman appeared and located the villains' shack with its control mechanism, crashed through the roof, banged their heads together and flew off with them. Using his x-ray vision, Superman saw there was dynamite inside the cruising icebergs and deduced the liner was being drawn to them by electromagnetic forces. He left the bad guys with the ship's captain, then lifted one iceberg and tossed it into another, resulting in a tremendous explosion. But there was still a third berg on the loose, so he picked up the ship and flew it over the iceberg to safety. He then zoomed back to the lethal iceberg and detonated it manually, returned to the ship, changed back to Clark Kent and joined Lois Lane for the remainder of the voyage. As usual, she wondered why Clark was never around when Superman saved the day.

Was there a leak somewhere in Combined Ops or the NRC chain of command? The head of civil engineering at the University of Manitoba, A.E. Macdonald, sent copies of the cartoon to the NRC in Ottawa, marked for the attention

The completed Habbakuk prototype floats on Patricia Lake, moored to the shore and disguised as a boathouse to hide it from possible enemy spies. JASPER YELLOWHEAD MUSEUM AND ARCHIVES

of C.J. Mackenzie, with the suggestion "they be taken seriously, in part." But there were no further stories in the press or the comics. Their bergship secret was safe. The similarity between what was happening on Patricia Lake and what was happening on a cartoon drawing board proved to be just coincidence. Fiction was imitating fact. But it gave them all a scare, and security was reviewed and tightened where possible.

As the work on the ice-ship prototype was drawing to

a close, Prime Minister Mackenzie King's diary entry for March 18, 1943, addressed the timing of the project to clear shipping lanes for convoys and described the war effort in England from his Canadian point of view:

> If we had enough aeroplanes to bomb Germany, the war should be ended through bombing but not likely otherwise. My own feeling is that the British are wise in seeking to get the maximum of planes and bring Germany to her knees through bombing, if possible, and not to attempt invasion until being absolutely sure of being able to get the necessary continued supplies, etc. across the Atlantic safely. This brings into consideration the habakkuk [sic] proposal which, to my mind, makes perfectly clear 1944, and which cannot in the nature of things be made of any real use until after the winter or 1943, or '44.

By March 22, 1943, when test and prototype results were coming in and being shared among those in British military circles with a need to know, a Combined Ops briefing note addressed to what extent the ship would be unsinkable and the effect the construction of such a ship would have on other production. It was concluded that "the lightness of the material now considered [pykrete] is such that the buoyancy of the ship should stand up to an unprecedented amount of punishment," and that building a bergship was a contracting task, not a shipbuilding one. The Ministry of Production considered that three ships could be built without seriously interfering with current war production, "bearing in mind that the cost of a ship would not be greatly in excess of a destroyer, this does not present a serious problem." The push was on to move from lab testing and prototypes to engineering design. But security aspects of the project were paramount, and "the need of the avoidance of discussion with persons who were not, to the certain knowledge of those concerned, properly and fully informed of its nature." While freedom of discussion between those engaged in scientific research was essential, reports on work in progress were to follow strict chain-of-command distribution rules.

With work at the different sites completed, final reports were prepared. The last task assigned to Montreal Engineering Company Limited by Mackenzie was to review all the reports summarizing investigations and results obtained. Not surprisingly they reported that ordinary ice was an unstable substance exhibiting both brittleness and plasticity as temperature and load varied. Reinforced ice beams were tested to their breaking point with results indicating that reinforced ice could be used as a structural material. The use of reinforcing bars of wood and steel, small-scale reinforcing using wood pulp or tree branches and a combination of the two were compared. Wood pulp worked and so did steel, which had the drawback of being expensive and in short supply. Large blocks of ice could be satisfactorily welded into structural forms by using water or slush as natural mortar, as long as temperatures remained at sub-zero. The work at Patricia Lake indicated the prototype could be built and floated and, by extrapolation, so could a larger vessel. The asphalt and charcoal aggregate used for insulation separated when poured in vertically, so pre-casting in horizontal slabs before erection was one possible solution.

Other lessons learned from the construction were that the full-size Habbakuk would need over 280,000 super-ice pykrete blocks and require manpower approaching 8,000 men over eight months. In addition, work could only be done in the short winter period. If the weather was mild, artificial freezing would be needed, which would divert scarce energy from other wartime industries. Shipbuilding costs alone were estimated to exceed $100 million, and no dry-dock facilities currently existed for such a gigantic vessel. The conclusion: obstacles were many, and the solutions few and costly. "Free" ice was not so free after all. It was decision time for Habbakuk. A summary report on the work in Canada ended with two recommendations: the project should either be dropped entirely or it must proceed vigorously with all necessary funding to meet war deadlines. There was no third option.

To top off all the test-result feedback, Mackenzie received a cryptic Canadian Pacific Telegraph message from Montreal Engineering Company:

Habbakuk consider construction within any reasonable predetermined time impracticable and in single season fantastic. Believe under present condition assembly personnel at site suggested to complete within say five years impracticable without compulsion already proven impossible enforce under our system government. All skilled labour would have to be drawn from other industries. Lack of knowledge characteristic principal material makes rapid development of design for even estimating purposes of doubtful value and plastic flow alone would appear condemn scheme. Consider any estimate cost speculative. Think your estimate lumber concrete pykrete void ice should be increased about fifty percent. Your overhead in total bears about correct proportion to specific items. Have no means checking mechanical items.

After this bombshell, Mackenzie had some serious decisions to make. On April 16, 1943, after the successful building of the 1:50 scale model, $1 million was allocated by the Canadian War Committee from the federal budget toward the cost of building a full-scale model Habbakuk. The cost of actually building an entire ice vessel would still be less than half the projected cost of a traditional vessel of equivalent immense size, of which there were none. The Patricia Lake prototype, made of pure ice, not pykrete, and all of the research to date had cost only $150,000. Meanwhile, over in London, the Royal Navy still expected to have an operational vessel by 1944. After all, the Canadians had successfully completed testing and the necessary raw materials were available to them. These included approximately 300,000 tons of wood pulp,

25,000 tons of fibreboard insulation, 35,000 tons of timber and 10,000 tons of steel. The Admiralty costed this out at £700,000. No problem!

By April 1943, the Admiralty was considering multiple uses for bergships, including serving as tankers, even though "the Prime Minister's original conception was a ship for operational use of aircraft." But the final decision rested "with the Canadians who will decide what can possibly be built." At this point, it was looking like nothing would be built either from pure ice or pykrete. Follow-up research at the lake site and other research centres continued to show how impractical the project would be in real life. And Mackenzie did not trust the cost estimates. The idea was as loony as he first thought. He wrote in his diary, "The construction aspects are almost overwhelming. The present time schedule certainly cannot be met and it is even possible that the thing can never be built."

Mackenzie ended the Patricia Lake project in May 1943. The prototype was stripped of everything reusable and the refrigeration unit turned off. The shell was allowed to sink to the bottom of the lake, although it took the entire summer to do so. The disappearing prototype took the Habbakuk concept with it to the bottom. Like the Allied command seeking to overcome the Atlantic Gap, Mackenzie had been caught in the gap between an idea and its implementation. He had to find the data that proved Habbakuk either worked or did not. No matter how hare-brained the scheme, he had no choice when the British and Canadian government came calling in wartime. He moved quickly, organized specialists, set up research sites, built a prototype to specifications within the imposed time frame and produced a realistic assessment of the costs and considerations of building a whole ship from ice.

Habbakuk wasn't the only NRC wartime ice project. Research was also conducted on ways to detect and prevent ice buildup on aircraft, and these studies extended to ice retardants for helicopters and ships. But while much practical information was gained from this wartime work in Canada, there were also dreamers. On May 25, 1943, the *Montreal Gazette* reported that an American consortium was proposing to make post-war high-speed passenger travel across the Atlantic safer and more relaxing by building three steel floating islands or "seadromes" of 64,000 tons, costing $10 million and spaced 800 miles (1,300 kilometres) apart. Each would stand 70 feet (21 metres) above water level and submerge 170 feet (52 metres) below, making them as steady as the mainland. They would have airport facilities and a hotel, so passengers could stop off and enjoy a "vacation at sea." They would be positioned outside fog and ice zones and would be self-propelled should they need to move. Construction would start after the war "just as soon as steel is available."

CHAPTER

6

Down the Drain

BY MID-1943, THE BATTLE OF THE ATLANTIC was going better for the Allies, so the need for a Habbakuk supercarrier or ice islands did not seem as important. Convoys were now crossing with minimal losses and the trans-Atlantic lifeline had been secured with technological advances like long-range aircraft and centimetric radar with 360-degree surveillance capability. Access to airbases in Iceland and Portugal's Azores had reduced the threat of U-boat wolf packs.

In March 1941, the push to break the communication codes used by U-boats in the Atlantic had been given a boost when the German armed trawler *Krebs* was captured off Norway complete with Enigma machines and code books. As more code books were captured, the Allies became better at discovering where U-boats were hunting and could endeavor to direct their own ships away from danger. But in February 1942, German innovations to naval Enigma machines had stymied the code breakers at Bletchley Park, and Allied losses in the Atlantic had increased. It was 10 months before the codes were broken, but by mid-December 1942, German naval messages were once again being read. However, this did not stop the carnage. It was an ongoing cat-and-mouse game. There were still many U-boats roaming the high seas, codes were continually being changed and Enigma machines upgraded, and U-boats could operate in silence without communicating for long periods of time. They were still a deadly foe.

In January 1943, when British and American leaders met at the Casablanca Conference (code name Symbol), Churchill and Roosevelt decided that complete defeat of the U-boats was their top priority. The liberation of Europe could not proceed until the Atlantic Gap was closed. Several initiatives were undertaken: more escort carrier groups were formed to provide protection for convoys; the new High Frequency Direction Finding ("Huff-Duff") system to pinpoint the direction of German submarine and ship radio signals was introduced; and 20 Very Long Range (VLR) Liberator aircraft were given to the Royal Canadian Air Force in Newfoundland to patrol for U-boats. By the middle of April 1943, that number had doubled to 41 VLR Liberators. At the same time, the British Royal Air Force (RAF) Coastal

Command had 28 anti-submarine squadrons active, and the number of escort ships was increasing, often allowing both an inner and outer protective cordon around convoys.

Even the weather cooperated. In April 1943, calmer conditions made both radar and Huff-Duff more effective, and North Atlantic losses fell by over 50 percent to 235,478 tons (39 ships that month). At the start of May, Germany still had approximately 60 U-boats hunting in the now reduced mid-Atlantic Gap. In a key attack, half were positioned across the path of a slow eastbound convoy, and 11 more waited further ahead. They engaged in a week-long running battle with the convoy and its escorts, sinking 12 merchant ships but at a cost of 7 U-boats. During the rest of the month, the wolf packs made a series of attacks that ultimately failed to inflict convoy losses. Conversely, U-boat casualties were mounting. By the end of May, 27 were lost in the North Atlantic, and nearly 100 had been sunk since January. VLR Liberators, not ice islands and Habbakuk, had closed the gap. There were now enough sea and air escorts accompanying the convoys to keep the wolf packs at bay. At the end of May, German U-boats withdrew from the Atlantic, signalling a decisive Allied victory.

Many of the key military leaders and scientists involved in pushing the bergship project forward and building the prototype now felt that even if a full-scale Habbakuk was possible, it was no longer strategically necessary. Besides, the complexity of building, insulating and refrigerating such a large structure would have required more time and manpower than the Allies could afford. And even though wood pulp was more plentiful than steel, there still weren't unlimited quantities. The amount needed to make pykrete for even one ice aircraft carrier would have shut down many newspapers in North America for lack of newsprint.

Churchill was not happy. He still wanted to go ahead with the project he had so energetically supported, and he was not giving up on his dream. Mackenzie made a trip to London after scuttling the Patricia Lake prototype, and on the evening of May 10, 1943, attended a small reception in his honour given by Canadian High Commissioner Vincent Massey. It was attended by Mountbatten and other high-ranking officers. Mackenzie used the occasion to inform them that an ice aircraft carrier could not possibly be built in 100 days, and furthermore, it was impossible to even meet a 1944 construction deadline. Mountbatten was disappointed but still held out hope that bergships could be used in the war effort, perhaps in the Pacific. Others told Mackenzie that his were the first sensible words they had heard about the Habbakuk project since it started. But committee meetings still continued with endless discussions on the properties of ice and pykrete, and designs and methods of construction. It was futile to continue meeting, but no bureaucrat wanted to make the final killing blow.

On June 10, 1943, Mackenzie went back to London for more meetings on the lingering Habbakuk project and attended a briefing with Churchill, Mountbatten, Bernal and other aides at 10 Downing Street. They were ushered into the prime minister's study, where he was busy working at his desk. Nobody said anything. When Churchill finished reading some papers, he faced the assembled group and said, "Well, Lord Louis, what is the situation?" When told no ice ship could possibly be ready by the end of 1943 or 1944, Churchill was very upset. He blustered. He ranted. He re-emphasized the need for floating platforms to provide fighter cover for landings in Norway or the Bay of Biscay, where German defences were not as strong as along the northern French coast. He still believed it was possible to cut a "lozenge of ice" 7 feet (2 metres) thick out of an Arctic icefield and use it as a landing platform. Even if such a platform lasted only one month, it would still be worth it.

Mountbatten then introduced Mackenzie, who proceeded to explain why Churchill's pet project of an iceberg aircraft carrier was not possible. As much as Canadians wanted the project to succeed and appreciated the great need, it was impossible to do what the prime minister desired. There was no readily accessible area with an ice thickness of 7 feet (2 metres), and it was not possible to build up ice at the rate of 8 to 10 feet (2.5 to 3 metres) per day, as Churchill believed. A 1944 time frame for a Habbakuk ship was impossible. Costs were excessive; labour was insufficient. The meeting lasted for over an hour, but nothing was resolved. It was agreed to set up yet another committee to further investigate alternative ice-support materials and mechanisms. It looked like Habbakuk would never die.

But the strategic environment was changing rapidly in favour of the Allies, and not just in the Atlantic. The Axis powers had been repulsed on land at El Alamein and Stalingrad (now St. Petersburg) and the US Marines were beginning to fight island-by-island in the Pacific theatre of war. The three major western Allied leaders agreed to a face-to-face meeting on key operational issues for the invasion of Europe, increased bombing of Germany and occupation of Italy. In August 1943, British prime minister Winston Churchill, American president Franklin Delano Roosevelt and Canadian prime minister Mackenzie King met to discuss strategy at the Citadelle at Quebec City, a massive star-shaped fortress on the highest point in the city, over-looking the St. Lawrence River, and at the nearby Chateau Frontenac. Accompanying his prime minister, Mountbatten took the opportunity to have a block of pykrete prepared by Montreal Engineering Company and delivered to the First Quebec Conference (code name Quadrant) along with a similar-sized block of pure ice. After the Canadian proto-type research at Patricia Lake, it was evident that Habbakuk faced supply and technical problems, not to mention costs estimated at $100 million just for the first ship. It was Britain's intent to get the Americans to assume financial responsibility for the project and convince them to use the bergship to enhance their war against Japan in the Pacific. A

William Lyon Mackenzie King, Franklin D. Roosevelt and Winston Churchill (seated left to right) pose with senior American and British military officers at the Citadelle during the Quebec Conference in August 1943. The empty chair on the left was for Josef Stalin, who refused to attend. NATIONAL FILM BOARD OF CANADA. PHOTOTHÈQUE/LIBRARY AND ARCHIVES CANADA C-001700

joint Anglo-American-Canadian committee with a secretariat at US Navy offices in Washington would oversee the project. And what better way to demonstrate the properties of ice and super-ice than to stage a live show-and-tell presentation.

During a break in the meeting of the Combined Chiefs of Staff at the Chateau Frontenac, Mountbatten had his block of pykrete and a block of pure ice wheeled in on a refrigerated trolley and uncovered in the middle of the conference room. Specialists and junior officers waited outside in the hallway to give their reports as each time slot on the agenda came around. Soon the senior officers came back in, closed the doors and settled down. They saw what appeared to be two blocks of ice in the centre of the room. Mountbatten explained that new materials being developed would change the duration of the war. To everyone's surprise he took out his service revolver and aimed at one of the blocks while warning onlookers to beware of splinters. Bang! At this range it was impossible to miss. Struck by his bullet, the ice shattered immediately. Nobody was really surprised—this is what ice does when hit with a sudden sharp force. But what was the point of all this, and what was Mountbatten going to do next? After all, he was still armed. Maybe the burdens of leadership had got to him and he needed a rest.

Mountbatten then said, "I shall fire at the block on the right and show you the difference." He took aim at the block of pykrete and fired. Another bang, but this time no flying shards of ice. The block remained intact, but the bullet ricocheted off the surface. Everyone in the room ducked for cover. The bullet passed through the pant leg of one of the officers in attendance and lodged in a wall. There was only a small dent in the pykrete block. With this demonstration he had proven his point and shown the strength and resilience of pykrete. Who could not find military uses for such a resilient material? The attendees outside were startled to hear two pistol shots ring out. "My God, the Americans are shooting the British!" somebody yelled. The military police rushed forward, flung open the doors and were stunned to see Mountbatten standing smiling, revolver still in hand, the centre of attention. All around him were melting ice shards and mayhem. Some officers were laughing, some were gesticulating wildly, but nobody remained seated around the conference table. Others in the room were just pleased to be alive.

Resisting all scientific arguments, Churchill still did not want to see the end of his pet project. He devised his own, less public spectacle at the Quebec Conference in order to convince Roosevelt to take over funding of a Habbakuk ice ship. Only the Americans had the large quantities of steel, the deep port and the deep pockets to make it a reality. If they agreed to participate, Britain would have access to American industry and the use of American shipyards. Another show-and-tell demonstration ensued. During a bilateral meeting with Roosevelt, Churchill had an ice cube dropped into a bowl between them on the table. Boiling water was poured into the bowl, and like the bathtub demonstration, the two men looked on as the ice cube melted. Then a cube of pykrete was dropped into another bowl and more boiling water poured in. Four eyeballs stared at one cube. Nothing happened. It retained its shape on top of the

British, Canadian and American Combined Chiefs of Staff meet at the Quebec Conference in August 1943. Among them is Louis Mountbatten, seated on the extreme left. NATIONAL FILM BOARD OF CANADA. LIBRARY AND ARCHIVES CANADA C-029467

hot water. "See," said Churchill, "it hasn't melted one bit." He then pulled out files and drawings marked "Most Secret" and proceeded to make his case for American involvement. He was very persuasive, and Roosevelt bought into the project before leaving the meeting, at least for the time being.

But the British Admiralty and the US military were no longer keen on the ice-ship idea and slow to follow the political direction. In true bureaucratic fashion, they threw up all kinds of objections. The ship would be too expensive on construction costs alone, they said. It was impossible to freeze the 1.7 million tons of pykrete needed per ship in just one Newfoundland winter. Canada did not have enough ice to build ice boats from mountain lake ice or from Arctic ice floes. Heat from the engines for the ship's propellers would melt the hull. Temperatures in the South Pacific would melt the whole ship.

Scientists tried to counter all the objections. They proposed one solution after another. If no ports were deep enough or no dry docks large enough, then they could make giant pykrete blocks, bond them together on top of a wooden raft, tow them out to sea and continue to build the ship there. Plus, they said, it would be less expensive than building the ship in dockyards already busy constructing conventional ships. Next, the Admiralty ordered that Habbakuk should be able to withstand 100-foot (30-metre) waves. But, it was pointed out, the bergship would only be used in the North Atlantic, and such waves only existed in the Antarctic. No matter, was the reply, all of His Majesty's ships had to be seaworthy in any ocean on which the Admiralty sailed, and they sailed on all the world's oceans. So the ship's design was changed to withstand such waves, and plans were finalized for the first ship of ice. Then came the manoeuvrability issue. How could Habbakuk be steered? Certainly, side engines with propellers would not be sufficient. Huge driveshafts and an immense rudder would have to be constructed, not out of wood but out of steel. This would escalate costs even more and further reduce the scarce supply of steel needed for other conventional warships and landing craft. One way or another, the Admiralty was determined that the Habbakuk project would be scuttled like the prototype on Patricia Lake.

In a letter dated September 23, 1943, Mackenzie wrote to General McNaughton:

> I spent two days at the Quebec Conference, to which I was invited by the British delegates, to consider Habakkuk [sic] and various other scientific matters which were being dealt with by the joint groups. I do not think that Habakkuk will become an actual reality but Mr. Churchill has been pressing the matter vigorously; while in Washington, he turned his guns on the American Navy, with the result that, after much resistance, they finally agreed to make a serious study of the problem and we are going to give them the results of the work done in Canada.

Back home after the Quebec Conference, more reservations set in. A joint Anglo-American-Canadian Habbakuk board had been struck, and C.J. Mackenzie was put in charge of the North American part of the project. The proposal on the table was for large-scale testing to be done in Canada and the United States, combined with ongoing laboratory work in England. Tests in Canada were to be supervised by Geoffrey Pyke. He was excited and prepared to leave immediately for Ottawa. Then he received a hand-written note from Mountbatten's chief of staff:

> I have disappointing news for you. CCO [Mountbatten, chief of Combined Operations] has telegraphed me to the following effect—Dean Mackenzie has just sent me a message to say that it is his considered opinion that if Pyke came out it would have a disastrous effect on American participation in this scheme, and he would have to advise his government accordingly. In the light of this uncompromising attitude I am afraid Pyke will have to stand down for the good of his own scheme. Consulted Bernal who entirely agrees. We are both so sorry. There is nothing more to be said, and I have suspended all activity in connection with booking your passage.

Geoffrey Pyke was crushed. He was left in charge of the lab work in England, but that was a poor consolation prize. After all, Habbakuk was his baby, the biggest idea he had given to Mountbatten and the War Office. Not wanting to be excluded entirely, he then proposed a less ambitious plan for pykrete vessels to be used in support of an amphibi-ous landing: a small warship 200 feet (61 metres) long by 50 feet (15 metres) wide with a single large naval gun tur-ret. This ship would be either self-powered or towed to the point of action. He also suggested the use of pykrete in breakwaters and landing stages for offloading troops and cargo. Max Perutz thought the ideas were practical and that research on pykrete had advanced sufficiently to allow the plan to be implemented. But it didn't happen. On D-Day—June 6, 1944—when the Allies confronted the enemy on the ground, liberated northwestern Europe and eventually ended the Nazi regime, they used a system of preformed concrete, not pykrete, breakwaters and landing stages, code-named "Mulberry," to provide temporary port facilities.

America continued to drag its feet on the Habbakuk project through the fall of 1943. They felt the technical problems would delay any launch until 1945 or later. Even though President Roosevelt and the US Navy had initially agreed to fund and take on the construction of a Habbakuk aircraft carrier on the premise it could be useful for their war in the Pacific, they never took action. Papers were shuffled, meetings were arranged and rearranged, then cancelled, and the project was quietly killed within the year. Their conventional aircraft-carrier fleet was now large enough to make an ice-composite carrier obsolete. In a memo to the British Chiefs of Staff, the Floating Islands Coordinating Committee recommended the Habbakuk Project "not be undertaken in the United Kingdom or the Empire." Perutz, who had been sent to Washington to work on the project, wrote in early 1944:

> The U.S. Navy finally decided that Habakkuk was a false prophet. One reason was the enormous amount of steel needed for the refrigeration plant that was to freeze the pykrete was greater than that needed to build the entire carrier of steel,

but the crucial argument was that the rapidly increasing range of land-based aircraft rendered floating islands unnecessary. The Canadians ordered that the prototype should be stripped of everything reusable and the refrigeration units turned off. The cold temperatures in Canada kept the boathouse frozen throughout the entire summer. In the fall of 1943 the once-revered Habbakuk project sank to the bottom of Patricia Lake with the melting prototype, taking her secrets with her.

Pyke did manage to wangle one last trip to Washington to advise the chief of US Naval Construction about further refinements for Habbakuk as part of the Anglo-American-Canadian board, but his recommendations fell on deaf ears. People "forgot" to tell him about meetings. Locations were changed at the last minute. His ideas were considered too radical, too difficult to implement. The concept of Habbakuk was sailing into the sunset. Pyke was frustrated, then astonished, to learn that he had been cut loose from his own project in America, too. Just as after Operation Plough, the Americans had no stomach for his eccentric ways and abrasive attitude and wanted him removed. It was small wonder—Pyke had sent a cable back to Mountbatten in London that read:

> HUSH MOST SECRET
> CIRCULATION RESTRICTED TO CHIEF OF COMBINED
>   OPERATIONS ONLY.
> CHIEF OF NAVAL CONSTRUCTION IS AN OLD WOMAN.
> SIGNED PYKE.

Objections to Habbakuk devolved into the ludicrous. There was the command obstacle. How could Habbakuk ever be commissioned, since no officer could command her? She was too large to be commanded by a lowly captain and no officer of higher rank could be assigned to her because she was, after all, only one ship. Late in 1943, the Habbakuk project was downgraded to a low-priority issue in Britain, for which Mountbatten listed several reasons, among them the great and growing demand for steel in aircraft and large ships; the introduction of long-range fuel tanks, which allowed British-based aircraft extra combat time over France and Europe; and the American preference for conventional aircraft carriers. And he went on to reiterate what was already known: Portugal's airfields in the Azores were now available to Allied aircraft covering the Atlantic Gap.

But most important of all, Mountbatten was no longer involved in Project Habbakuk. Churchill had appointed him Supreme Allied Commander, South-East Asia Command (SEAC). In October 1943, Mountbatten departed COHQ for his Far East assignment. On his last day in charge of Combined Ops, he wrote this tribute to Pyke:

Dear Pyke,

I am leaving C.O.H.Q. today and feel that I must write to thank you for all you have done for me during the past eighteen months.

You must feel proud to think that the force [Devil's

Brigade/1st Special Service Force], the creation of which you originally suggested to me in March 1942, has become such a vital necessity in the coming stage of the war that General Eisenhower and the C-in-C, Middle East are vying between them to try to obtain the services of this force, probably the most bold and imaginative scheme of this war, and owing its inception to you. It is still too secret to refer to it in a letter of this nature, but one day I feel that you will be able to look with pride on this child of your imagination.

My Chief Planners told me that you have on more than one occasion contributed valuable suggestions to their plans and in general I consider that the original thoughts which you have contributed to this Headquarters have been of the utmost value to the war effort.

I am arranging for you to help the Director of Plans, Admiralty after I leave here,

Yours sincerely,
Louis Mountbatten

Naval architects directed by Bernal continued working on variations of Pyke's original concept in a desperate attempt to pump some life back into the project. In the end, they produced three alternative Habbakuks: Habbakuk I, made of wood (which was quickly rejected); Habbakuk II, a slow, self-propelled monster vessel made of pykrete with steel reinforcement (this version was closest to the COHQ's preferred model); and Habbakuk III, a smaller but faster version of Habbakuk II (this niche was already filled by conventional vessels).

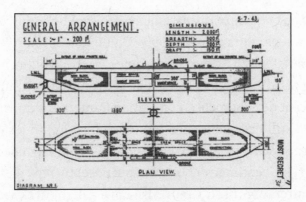

This diagram of Habbakuk was among secret British documents on the project declassified in 1982. NATIONAL ARCHIVES OF THE UK, KEW

When Bernal was asked about potential bomb damage to Habbakuk III, he suggested that a certain amount of deck covering might be ripped off but could be repaired by some unspecified kind of flexible matting. Bomb damage to the central portion of the ship would be more difficult to deal with, though the roof over the aircraft hangars would be capable of withstanding 1-ton (1,000-kilogram) bombs. Bernal considered that no one could say whether the larger Habbakuk II was a practical proposition until a large-scale model could be completed and tested in Canada in the spring of 1944. He had no doubts about the suitability of pykrete as a useable material for a vessel, but significant "constructional and navigational" difficulties remained to be overcome. The planners' final design for Habbakuk II gave the bergship a displacement of 2.2 million tons. Steam turbo-generators would supply 33,000 horsepower (25,000 kilowatts) for 26 externally mounted electric motors in separate nacelles or pods located away from the hull (in spite of recent developments, conventional internal ship engines would still have generated too much heat for an ice craft). Its armaments would have included 40 dual-barrelled 4.5-inch (11.4-centimetre) DP (dual-purpose) turrets, plus light anti-aircraft guns. It would also have a flight deck with up to 150 twin-engine bombers or fighters housed below on the hangar deck

The final Habbakuk board meeting was held in December 1943. It was then announced that, "The large Habbakuk II made of pykrete has been found to be impractical because of the enormous production resources required and technical difficulties involved." Pyke's dream was over, although other ideas for floating islands were still under consideration, such as welding Liberty ships (quickly and easily built freighters transporting troops, arms and material) or landing craft together, referred to as Project Tentacle in military jargon. A separate project to build pykrete freighters which could have carried eight Liberty ships as cargo was proposed but rejected as unnecessary.

A press release issued by the NRC in 1946, "Account of the Habbakuk Project (iceberg ship)," came to the following conclusions:

A scheme of this magnitude undertaken in wartime is necessarily a gamble and was recognized to be so from the start. Its failure, therefore, only serves to demonstrate the inevitable cost of pursuing a policy involving the backing of new and ingenious ideas. Such a policy appears fully justifiable in war. In actual fact, the effort involved was mainly confined to research, and this research may well in the long run provide its own justification, in that valuable information has now been obtained regarding the properties of ice and the effects of its reinforcement. This study throws light on many problems other than those referring to ice, particularly on the mechanism of brittleness and creep. The material collected and the research initiated will provide an admirable basis for further ice engineering research, useful to all countries with severe winters. Furthermore, the research concerned with ship form and construction may also prove of value where they enlarge our knowledge of the performance of vessels of unusual sizes and shapes.

All the top-secret classified material about the project, mostly progress reports and final recommendations from the work done in Canada, were locked in a filing-cabinet drawer at the NRC in Ottawa. According to Dr. Lorne W. Gold, the council research scientist in ice engineering and construction entrusted with their care in 1953, they were "an excellent record of a major part of what was probably the largest research and development program on ice carried out to that time." He did not find anything in the papers to justify a top-secret classification, but an attempt to declassify the material was unsuccessful. The official reason was that declassification could only be authorized by the individual who initiated the project, and nobody would acknowledge that role. Subsequent declassification attempts were equally unsuccessful, so the records stayed safe and secure in Dr. Gold's office. The NRC only agreed to release its records when the eight crates of records in England were declassified following the mandatory 35-year waiting period and were made available for consultation at the Public Records Office in Kew.

In essence, the Habbakuk experience could be summed up as "the project succeeded but not the objective. Much useful knowledge was gained but no ship sailed the seas." The research, experiments, tests and prototype proved the concept was sound, but the operational target to launch a flotilla of Habbakuk-style ships was not feasible in terms of cost or timing, nor would such a ship be useful in war today. However, the initiative did open up a whole field of study on the properties of ice and collected new data on the contours of super-ship hulls, wave action, refrigeration, northern airfields and ice highways.

CHAPTER

7

Repercussions

THE IMMENSE STRATEGIC ADVANTAGE of building bergships to close the Atlantic Gap, combined with a lack of
knowledge about the properties of ice as a construction
material, muted initial opposition in military circles to
the Habbakuk scheme. But the fatal flaws in the project
eventually were too great for even its most ardent proponents to overcome. The shift from cutting bergships out of
glaciers and ice floes to reinforcement with pykrete vastly
complicated Pyke's original concept. Costs escalated astro-
nomically with the discoveries that natural freezing would
be much too slow for the ever-increasing size of the vessel and that artificial refrigeration was needed to produce
required amounts of reinforced ice. The size of the harbour

and dry docks needed to build the ship, the estimated quantity of timber, steel and machinery, plus the 8,000-person workforce necessary for construction meant the project was no longer an elegantly simple "ice island." In recommending to Mackenzie that involvement in Habbakuk cease, R.E. Chadwick, head of the NRC construction team in Canada, declared "the project has lost all prospect of being either cheap or easy to construct." The huge cost and impossible time frame caused the bergship concept to melt away.

While most opponents of the Habbakuk scheme were muzzled by the Official Secrets Act and kept their opinions to themselves, others tried to speak out but found the chain of command unreceptive to dissent. From early 1943, Sir Charles Goodeve, assistant controller of research and development for the Admiralty during the Second World War, expressed reservations about the feasibility of Habbakuk. War had been fought by steel and explosives, aluminum and electrons, but ice? It may be hard, but it has no strength. Goodeve was alarmed when leaders were swayed by "long-haired scientists" and the "magnetic personality of the inventor." Those who spoke out against the scheme, whom Goodeve called "voices of reason," were labelled obstructionist by the promoters of Habbakuk, who had the ear of the prime minister.

Goodeve found the idea of ice ships absurd and believed that the effort invested in them would be better spent winning the war by conventional means. He was on the side of the scientists and engineers working on developments like radar and tank-landing craft. In a post-war article, he pointed out that the large amount of wood pulp required to make pykrete would have significantly affected paper production around the world. He also claimed that since each Habbakuk ship would require 40,000 tons of cork insulation, thousands of miles of steel tubing for brine circulation in the refrigeration system and four power stations, those resources could produce greater benefit elsewhere, such as in manufacturing conventional ships of more effective fighting power than the slow, ponderous Habbakuk. According to Sir Charles, those in charge of war programs had "the Hobson's Choice of either fighting this absurdity or of ignoring it as far as possible"—that is to say, no choice at all. His reference was to having a supposedly free choice when only one possible option is actually offered; in other words, take it or leave it. (The phrase is said to have originated with Thomas Hobson [1544–1631], a livery-stable owner in England who, to rotate the use of his horses, offered customers the choice of either taking the horse in the stall nearest the door or taking no horse at all.)

Goodeve derisively referred to the Habbakuk project as a fantasy and went on to say:

> At one stage they [the proponents of ice] thought it would be a good idea to send the whole party to Canada, where the winter might cool its ardour. The Canadians were sensible

people; they would get this monstrous fantasy under control. But ahead of the team went the message: this was Canada's opportunity to play a part in history! Far up in the Rocky Mountains a lake was chosen . . . a camp was built . . . an experimental model was constructed. Hundreds of skilled designers were put to work all over the country designing refrigerating plants, remotely operated electric propulsion motors, etc., they knew not for what. Came the spring, and with it one conclusion from the trials, *ice melts*.

But, he continued, "all would have been well if it hadn't happened that at this moment one of the many parties detailed off for research into the problems of Habbakuk discovered that ice could be given some strength by incorporating a large amount of paper-making pulp in the water before freezing." Next, Goodeve took aim with gusto and exaggeration at the proponents of pykrete, adding:

A bullet fired at it went in so smoothly that the ice reformed behind it. The followers were elated and called this material Pykrete in honour of their leader. It is not only unsinkable, but it is self-healing against bullets, bombs and torpedoes! Never mind if we have to reduce all the Allied newspapers to letter size . . . But there was one obstacle that even research and faith could not overcome. Great Britain hadn't the resources to build even one Habbakuk. Fortunately a decision was made not to wait for Habbakuk and the great three-power committee [UK-US-Canada] was never convened . . . But at such high altitudes came a new discovery. Not only does ice melt, it evaporates! And so did Habbakuk.

In a scientific paper presented in 1947, Max Perutz, who had thoroughly investigated pykrete characteristics and applications in construction, acknowledged that the Habbakuk project presented a challenge. In his estimation, some 1,700,000 tons of the stuff were required to build one ship. This would have required a production plant covering 100 acres (40 hectares). Manufacturing the amount of piping and refrigerating apparatus needed would have drained the capacity of North American industries. But he gives other reasons why the project was abandoned in early 1944, mentioning improvements in aircraft performance and range over the Atlantic, and the successful island-hopping campaign of the Americans in the Pacific, which made the invasion of Japan seem possible without the support of large floating airbases. Also, the longer runways needed for newer aircraft meant any flight-deck extension on Habbakuk still would have been insufficient.

From the point of view of the war effort alone, "the research and planning spent on the bergship project proved to have been wasted. Yet . . . this daring venture came to fascinate men's minds and was welcomed as a possible solution for one of the most difficult military problems facing the Allies. The secrecy of the project was so great that most of the workers engaged on pykrete research had no idea of its purpose." Speaking about the overall knowledge gain from Habbakuk, Perutz said, "The volume of first-rate data produced within a period of six months in this country and in Canada under the pressure of war far exceeded the total volume of reliable work that had been done before on the mechanical properties of ice itself."

While a great amount of innovative thinking and precise testing was directed at the ice-ship concept, the NRC concluded "the death of the Habbakuk project was in effect determined by strategic, technical and economic considerations." Just because a material is cheap and plentiful does not mean that the labour needed to work that material is equally cheap and plentiful. If a full-size Habbakuk had been built, some historians believe it would have been the second-most important technological development of the Second World War after the atomic bomb. Certainly it was initially thought to be as important to the war effort as Little Boy, code name of the uranium atomic bomb dropped on Hiroshima on August 6, 1945, and Fat Man, the plutonium atomic bomb detonated over Nagasaki on August 9, 1945, both of which were products of the US-based Manhattan Project. At the Quebec Conference where Project Habbakuk had been given a feeble reprieve, the leaders had signed the Quebec Agreement outlining the terms of the UK-US-Canada partnership in the development of atomic bomb and nuclear technology. America's secret weapon would end the war with Japan not with ice but with fire.

Geoffrey Pyke was granted the right to patent pykrete in the United States, but he never filed an application. Still, the Mountbatten-Pyke collaboration continued. In his new assignment as Supreme Allied Commander, Southeast Asia Command, working with the Americans to liberate Japanese-held territory, Mountbatten asked Pyke to bend his brain to a critical problem in the Pacific theatre of war. Allied ships had to unload essential supplies in isolated, makeshift ports, and new roads had to be pushed through jungle swamps and over mountains to reach the front lines. Early on, the only transport vehicle was pack mule. Supply lines were stretched to the breaking point. Pyke wrote out a lengthy proposal to construct "power-driven rivers," which Professor Bernal paraphrased as "essentially the use of pipelines to carry military and other stores in cylindrical containers along with oil or other liquid inside the pipe." Pyke suggested 6-inch (15-centimetre) pipes for smaller items and 2-foot (0.6-metre) pipes for larger items, and the pipes could be extended as military front lines advanced. Pyke pointed out that his idea of sending objects through a pipeline was not new. Cleaning brushes had been carried by liquid pressure through oil pipelines in the United States back in 1930. But he was the first to propose tube transportation or hydraulic capsule pipelines (HCP) as a way to transport goods.

Following up in a June 1944 memo, Pyke amplified on his proposal: "Owing to its superficial appearance of novelty and imagination, I abstained . . . from all mention of the possibility of using them [power-driven rivers] for the transport of troops." Pyke was well aware that the ridicule such a project would attract could undermine support, but continued, "The idea of transporting human beings inside the pipe has a slightly imaginative and speculative quality about it." The problems of providing oxygen to troops in transit, claustrophobia, high pressures, speed and cost all concerned Pyke, but as usual, he left the details of solving such issues for others to address. The ultimate problem was the vulnerability of people pipelines to enemy attack. His idea was never developed because such pipelines would have to be laid on roadbeds, which came right back to the problem of building new roads through jungles and over mountains.

After the Second World War, Pyke continued his flow of ideas to make a better peacetime world. He suggested the problem of supplying energy for rail transportation in post-war Europe could be solved by propelling railway cars by human muscle power. Some 20 to 30 men pedalling a bicycle-like mechanism could propel a cyclo-tractor that would save the coal consumed by a locomotive doing similar work. No takers stepped forward to commercialize the concept. Pyke continued to write and talk on radio about his innovative ideas. "The underlying issue of our time," he wrote, "is whether our civilization can be reformed or whether, for progress, a revolution is essential." He also campaigned against the death penalty as punishment for any crime.

But the more Pyke thought about making a better world,

the more pessimistic he became about the future. He was widely mocked in the mainstream media and was the subject of derision in socialist papers. A sense of gloom descended over him. Depressed by the Cold War and the state of the world, in the evening of February 28, 1948, Pyke shaved his beard and downed a bottle of sleeping pills. His landlady found his body the next morning. His corpse was cremated. No service was held. No grave marker was erected.

An obituary in the *Times* noted, "The death of Geoffrey Pyke removes one of the most original if unrecognized figures of the present century." Mountbatten called Pyke "the most unusual and provocative man I have ever met." Professor Bernal commented that Pyke had "remained always the knight-errant, from time to time gathering round him a small band of followers but never a leader of big movements. Because of the very greatness of his ideas most of his life was one of frustration and disappointment, but he has left behind to all who knew him and were indirectly affected by him the vision he created for making all things possible."

Epilogue

LORD LOUIS MOUNTBATTEN WAS NICKNAMED "Supremo" by his staff when he served as Supreme Allied Commander, South East Asia Command, repelling the Japanese offensive to India and overseeing the re-conquest of Burma. In September 1945, he received the Japanese surrender at Singapore, and he remained with South East Asia Command until 1946. In 1947, Mountbatten was appointed the last viceroy of India with a mandate to oversee the end of British administration there. For his services during the Second World War and in India, he was raised to the British peerage and created Viscount Mountbatten of Burma in 1946 and Earl Mountbatten of Burma the following year. He continued to occupy the position of Governor-General in

India under the new constitution until 1948. Mountbatten served his final posting in the Admiralty as First Sea Lord from 1955–59. He departed his most excellent world on August 27, 1979, at the age of 79, murdered by Irish Republican Army (IRA) terrorists when his boat was blown up in Donegal Bay, County Sligo, Ireland, while he was on vacation.

After the end of the Second World War, some interest remained in using ice islands for scientific and industrial purposes. In 1946, aerial photographs showed islands of ice several miles in diameter and well over 165 feet (50 metres) thick floating in the Arctic Ocean. One, named T-3 or Fletcher's Ice Island, was used as a platform for ocean-ographic and atmospheric observations as it moved around for several years, finally making its way along the east coast of Greenland into the Atlantic Ocean where it melted. Islands of such size regularly break off the ice shelf attached to Ward Hunt Island in the Canadian Arctic Archipelago. In 1984, an ice island 4.3 miles long by 1.9 miles wide and 144 feet thick (7 kilometres long by 3 kilometres wide and 44 metres thick) in the Arctic Basin was promptly claimed by Canada and named Hobson's Choice. It also became a base for scientific observations.

In 1957, North Rankin Nickel Mines sought informa-tion on pykrete to construct pit supports and a pier on the western shore of Hudson Bay, but not all Habbakuk-related information had been declassified at that time, and neither the British nor Canadian governments would open their sealed files. There were also preliminary discussions regarding an ice boat that could double as a refrigerator, thus revolutionizing the fishing industry, but those ideas were never pursued.

With the discovery of oil and gas in the Arctic Archipelago, companies now use ice islands as drilling platforms to sink exploratory holes and are investigating micro-reinforced ice as a buffer against the force winter sea ice exerts on offshore drilling structures.

The December 17, 1960, issue of *Maclean's* addressed Operation Habbakuk as "The Weirdest Secret Weapon of the War," outlining "how Geoffrey Pyke sold Winston Churchill a vision of unsinkable carriers made of unmeltable ice" that was seriously considered by the Combined Chiefs of Staff but later abandoned in favour of other options. In 2009, the Discovery Channel television program *Mythbusters* built a small boat out of modified pykrete (they used shredded newspaper instead of wood pulp) and successfully steered it through Alaskan coastal waters at a speed of 25 miles (40 kilometres) per hour. Further tests proved it to be bullet resistant, stronger than ice and slower to melt. In 2010, the popular science BBC-TV program *Bang Goes the Theory* attempted to recreate a pykrete boat using 11,000 pounds (5,000 kilograms) of hemp-reinforced water that had been frozen solid in a cold-storage warehouse. They launched their icy craft at Portsmouth, a naval dockyard on

the south coast of England. The hull began to melt immediately, and they sank before leaving the harbour. The crew
did not go down with their ship, but were happily rescued.

In the 1970s, decades after the Habbakuk prototype was
scuttled at Patricia Lake, divers found a jumble of twisted
metal piping used in the ductwork and a large quantity of
asphalt, either in slabs or still clinging to framing material.
The cold lake water had preserved much of the wood and construction materials. Pieces of electrical wire were present but
no vermiculite, even though two boxcars of this substance
had been delivered to the worksite in 1943. The protective
roof of the boathouse was missing, but all four walls were
present with one still upright. The refrigeration chamber was
intact, but all machinery had been removed from the prototype before setting it adrift in 1944. The remains are there to
this day, although they lie near a steep underwater cliff and
could slide over into the abyss and disappear forever.

In 1988, a plaque was placed by the Alberta Underwater
Archaeological Society on the bottom of Patricia Lake at
the remains of the scale model. It proclaims the site an
underwater historical resource. Another commemora-
tive plaque was erected by the National Research Council
and Parks Canada on the lakeshore near the site in 1989.
Drivers can pull off the road and admire the mountain
vista, while under the reflective waters of Patricia Lake one
of the most unusual experiments of the Second World War
rests in its watery grave.

Timeline

September 23, 1942 Geoffrey Pyke sends a memo about Habbakuk ships made from ice to Louis Mountbatten at COHQ.

December 5, 1942 Mountbatten forwards the idea via memo to Prime Minister Winston Churchill.

December 11, 1942 Churchill sends a memo to the Chiefs of Staff Committee expressing interest in floating ice islands and bergships.

January 8, 1943 British scientists submit a report to the Habbakuk Committee noting ice is a cheap, natural material but has problems when used in construction. American scientists experiment with ways to reinforce ice.

January 28, 1943 As part of Canada's war effort, the NRC undertakes to conduct ice-engineering research in Ottawa, Montreal and with universities and at national parks in western Canada.

February 12, 1943 The NRC reports progress in ongoing tests on tensile strength of steel, wood and ice.

February 15, 1943 Outdoor ice work begins at Banff and on the Habbakuk prototype at Patricia Lake, near Jasper. Meanwhile, lab work on pykrete is being undertaken at the Smithfield Market in London.

March 1, 1943 Pyke and Bernal arrive in Ottawa and leave with Mackenzie on a tour of work sites in western Canada.

March 4, 1943 Pyke, Bernal and Mackenzie arrive in Saskatoon.

March 8, 1943 Pyke, Bernal and Mackenzie arrive at Lake Louise.

Timeline

April 1, 1943 A report on the work in Canada recommends the project should either be dropped or must proceed vigorously to meet war deadlines.

August 17–24, 1943 Mountbatten demonstrates the resilient qualities of pykrete at the Quebec Conference (code name Quadrant) and a Joint Habbakuk Board under the US Navy is proposed to investigate using bergships in the Pacific for the war with Japan.

December 14, 1943 The NRC officially ends Project Habbakuk.

December 16, 1943 Pykrete ships are deemed too costly and not feasible without detracting from other war priorities, so the project is dropped.

January 27, 1944 In a memo to the British Chiefs of Staff, the Floating Islands Coordinating Committee recommends the Habbakuk Project "not be undertaken in the United Kingdom or the Empire."

1982 Habbakuk documents are fully declassified.

1988 The Alberta Underwater Archaeological Society marks the sunken remains of the Habbakuk prototype with an underwater plaque.

1989 The NRC and National Parks Service erect a plaque on the shore of Patricia Lake commemorating the Second World War events that took place there.

Selected Bibliography

Brown, Andrew. *J.D. Bernal: The Sage of Science*. Oxford: Oxford University Press, 2005.

Costello, John, and Terry Hughes. *The Battle of the Atlantic*. London: Collins, 1977.

Gold, Lorne W. *The Canadian Habbakuk Project*. Cambridge: International Glaciological Society, 1990.

Lampe, David. *Pyke: The Unknown Genius*. London: Evans Brothers, 1959.

Parsons, Zack. *My Tank is Fight!* New York: Citadel Press Books, 2006.

Perutz, Max. "A Description of the Iceberg Aircraft Carrier." *Journal of Glaciology* 1, no. 3 (1948): 95–104.

Perutz, Max. *Wish I Made You Angry Earlier*. Oxford: Oxford University Press, 2002.

Pickover, Clifford A. *Strange Brains and Genius: The Secret Lives of Eccentric Scientists and Madmen*. New York: Harper Perennial, 1999.

Pyke, Geoffrey. *To Ruhleben—And Back*. London: Constable and Company, 1916.

Richmond, Randy, and Tom Villemaire. *Colossal Canadian Failures*. Toronto: Dundurn Press, 2002.

Rohmer, Richard. *E. P. Taylor: The Biography of Edward Plunkett Taylor*. Halifax: Goodread Biographies, 1983.

Thistle, Mel. *The Mackenzie-McNaughton Wartime Letters*. Toronto: University of Toronto Press, 1975.

Selected Bibliography

Toews, J.A. *Alternative Service in Canada during World War II.* Winnipeg: University of Manitoba, 1957.

Ziegler, Philip. *Mountbatten: The Official Biography.* London: Sterling Publishing, 2001.

Index

Index

Acknowledgements

No work is ever created in isolation. There are numerous inputs, influences, interpretations, experiences and events that flavour the finished product. I especially appreciate the research help provided by Robert Mercier, which included access to his extensive library right here in Ottawa. Living in the resource-rich environment of the National Capital Region, with its museums, universities, and libraries, plus Library and Archives Canada, is an experience any taxpaying writer would savour.

I would like to thank Lesley Reynolds for her editing expertise, as well as Richard Bourgeois-Doyle of the National Research Council, Corporate Governance, and Steven Leclair of the National Research Council, Content Access Services, for their assistance in sourcing documentation and illustrations. I would also like to thank Dora Winter of Library and Archives Canada, Document Consultation Services, for images in their collection.

About the Author

L. D. Cross is an Ottawa writer and member of the Professional Writers Association of Canada (PWAC) and the Canadian Authors Association (CAA). Her business and lifestyle articles have appeared in Canada and the United States. Her publication credits include magazines such as *WeddingBells, Home Business Report, Legion Magazine, Profit Magazine, enRoute, AmericanStyle, Fifty-Five Plus, Health Naturally, Antiques!, Airborn* and *This Country Canada* as well as the *Globe and Mail* newspaper. Her creative non-fiction has been recognized by the International Association of Business Communicators (IABC), Ottawa Chapter, EXCEL Awards for features and editorial writing, as well as the National Mature Media Awards for her writing about seniors. In 2011, her book *The Underground Railroad: The Long Journey to Freedom in Canada* received the inaugural Ontario Historical Society Huguenot Award honouring "the best book published in Ontario in the past three years which has brought public awareness to the principles of freedom of conscience and freedom of thought."

Cross is the author of other books in the Amazing Stories series, including *Ottawa Titans: Fortune and Fame in the Early Days of Canada's Capital*; *Spies in Our Midst: The Incredible Story of Igor Gouzenko, Cold-War Spy*; *The Quest for the Northwest Passage: Exploring the Elusive Route Through Canada's Arctic Waters*; and *Treasure Under the Tundra: Canada's Arctic Diamonds*. She is also a co-author of *Inside Outside: In Conversation with a Doctor and a Clothing Designer* and *Marriage is a Business*.

More Great Books in the Amazing Stories Series

Treasure Under the Tundra

Canada's Arctic Diamonds

L.D. Cross

print ISBN 978-1-926936-08-6
ebook ISBN 978-1-926936-10-9

It is said that the sparkle from Canadian diamonds mimics the magnificent and seductive radiance of the northern lights. Yet until 1991, no one thought diamonds could even be found in Canada—no one except Chuck Fipke and Stu Blusson, who uncovered diamond-rich kimberlite in the Barrens at Point Lake in the Northwest Territories. Their spectacular find caused great excitement in international diamond circles and sparked the largest claim-staking rush in Canada since the 1896 Klondike gold rush. Here is the dramatic tale of two determined geologists who risked all and triumphed over incredible odds.

Visit heritagehouse.ca to see the entire list of books in this series.

More Great Books in the Amazing Stories Series

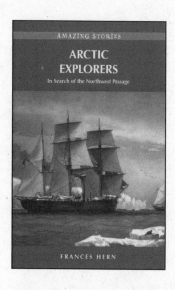

Arctic Explorers

In Search of the
Northwest Passage

Frances Hern

print ISBN 978-1-926613-29-1
ebook ISBN 978-1-926936-13-0

The search for the Northwest Passage is a saga of hardship, tragedy and mystery. For over 400 years, the elusive, ice-choked Arctic waterway has been sought and travelled by daring men seeking profit and glory but often finding only a desperate struggle for survival. Spanning the centuries from Elizabethan privateer Martin Frobisher to RCMP officer Henry Larsen, the intrepid captain of the *St. Roch*, these stories of high adventure reveal why the Northwest Passage has gripped the imaginations of generations of explorers and lured them to its treacherous waters.

Visit heritagehouse.ca to see the entire list of books in this series.

More Great Books in the Amazing Stories Series

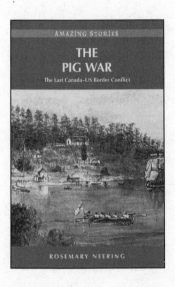

The Pig War

The Last Canada–US Border Conflict

Rosemary Neering

print ISBN 978-1-926936-01-7
ebook ISBN 978-1-926936-63-5

On May 15, 1859, an American settler on San Juan Island shot a pig belonging to the Hudson's Bay Company. This seemingly insignificant act almost triggered an all-out war between Britain and the United States on the northwest coast of North America. At stake was control of the strategically located San Juan Islands, and as both sides mustered their forces, conflict seemed inevitable. This lively account of the border dispute now known as the Pig War traces the events that led to the standoff in the San Juans and brings to life the memorable characters who played leading roles in the drama.

Visit heritagehouse.ca to see the entire list of books in this series.

More Great Books in the Amazing Stories Series

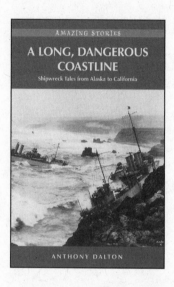

A Long, Dangerous Coastline

Shipwreck Tales from Alaska to California

Anthony Dalton

print ISBN 978-1-926613-73-4
ebook ISBN 978-1-926936-11-6

On September 8, 1923, seven US Navy destroyers rammed into jagged rocks on the California coast. Twenty-three sailors died that night. Five years earlier, the Canadian Pacific passenger ship *Princess Sophia* steamed into Vanderbilt Reef in Alaska's Lynn Canal. When she sank, she took 353 people to their deaths. From San Francisco's fog-bound Golden Gate to the stormy Inside Passage of British Columbia and Alaska, the magnificent west coast of North America has taken a deadly toll. Here are the dramatic tales of ships that met their end on this treacherous coastline—including *Princess Sophia*, *Benevolence*, *Queen of the North* and others.

Visit heritagehouse.ca to see the entire list of books in this series.